ADVANCE PRAISE

"For twenty years, I have trusted Kris Holmes as a career advisor and mentor. Her advice has helped me as I've built my career, and I recommend her book, Ignite Your Career, to anyone looking to build a successful career doing what they love."

"Having reviewed a hundred-plus career self-help books, I say don't put this one down! Kris Holmes' recruiting experience cuts through the job hunt noise into the hidden gems of accessing company culture and finding 'best fit.' Like none other, she'll convince you to cancel that 'you should be' advice. She leads you to amplify natural aptitudes as your competitive advantage to find your flow, voice, and most lasting rewards. Turn pages to experience a personal career coach, a mentor, and a recruiter's eyes."

"Ignite Your Career represents a must-read career development book that is useful for college students determining their career direction, and young professionals facing career decisions. Kris Holmes provides an incredibly practical and well-defined approach to career path optimization delivered in an engaging style."

"Kris brings such a simple, yet comprehensive step-by-step approach to what many of us find so overwhelming and daunting—'what should I do with my life?' Share this book with anyone that doesn't know where to begin in forging their professional path or those that are considering a change from their current one."

—SUZANNE MCIVER, ASSOCIATE DIRECTOR, EMPLOYER RELATIONS WASHINGTON UNIVERSITY

"As a training, recruiting, and career services professional, I believe Ignite Your Career is an easily digestible read that encourages reflection and how-to skills to navigate your work life journey."

—KRISTEN MCCORMACK, CAREER ADVISOR AT A LEADING LIBERAL ARTS COLLEGE

"We spend so much time in schools asking students to focus on the journey rather than the destination. It is wonderful to find a resource for young people that lets them think about the destination and gives them all of the practical necessities to get to that destination without undermining all that is so valuable in a meaningful and well-examined life."

—ANDY ABBOT, HEAD OF SCHOOL, JOHN BURROUGHS HIGH SCHOOL, ST. LOUIS MO

"The world is absurd; we are forced to make profound decisions that will impact our life's direction and standard of living for decades to come long before we are emotionally equipped to do

so. I never know what to say to students, but thank God Kris Holmes does. Her book is wise, engaging, and more importantly, set up to guide you step by step as you navigate that first job, that first decade of work experience, and to do so by staying true to yourself."

—DANNY CAHILL, PRESIDENT/OWNER AT HOBSON ASSOCIATES AND AUTHOR OF *AGING DISGRACEFULLY*

"Ignite Your Career is a book that I wish had been in the library of my college-age self. Kris Holmes provides keen insight for anyone entering the workforce or evaluating their career journey; this is a must-read."

—ROB BOWERMAN, PRESIDENT PINNACLE SOCIETY AND THE BOWERMAN GROUP

"Wow! I wish I had this book in college, or even high school. Ignite Your Career would have helped me make much better, more informed, and more rewarding career and life choices without having to learn these the hard way."

—DOMINIC IACONO, MANAGING DIRECTOR, KIMBERLY-CLARK—HONG KONG AND FORMER DIRECTOR OF MARKETING PROCTER & GAMBLE

"Ignite Your Career will help you...Right. Now. Careers are a journey, and there is great value in understanding your starting point—your interests, not merely what others say you should do...and importantly, your inherent skills. Kris has years of experience guiding exceptional people toward the right 'fit.'

Ignite Your Career is packed with clear and concise guidance and sage advice that you will not find elsewhere. Lots of wisdom in these pages!"

—TYLER JOHNSTON, OPERATING PARTNER, HUMMINGBIRD BRANDS, LLC AND FORMER CMO DREYER'S GRAND ICE CREAM

"Ignite Your Career is an easy and informative read for anyone getting ready to start their career. I wish I could take this book and jump into a time machine and arrive 20 years ago. Kris Holmes has worked magic by demystifying career planning and sharing steps to help land your dream job."

—ARMANDO GARZO, SVP SALES AND MARKETING, YOUSCIENCE

"Ignite Your Career is the career playbook I wish I had when I graduated. It will help any graduate structure the ambiguous and important choices they face about what to do next. I was lucky enough to be coached by Kris early in my career—her book is the next best thing."

—BRAD JOHNSON, CHIEF COMMERCIAL OFFICER, HUNGRY PLANET

"Ignite Your Career is an insightful guide that simplifies and demystifies career planning and gives a road map for how to go after your dream job. Read this book! It will help you make smart decisions, focus you on pursuing your long-term goals, and give you the tools to attain them."

—DOUG PEARSON, EXECUTIVE COACH

"Thank you, Kris, for taking your decades of experience and distilling insights into a readable and useful 'how to manual' to get the most out of ourselves by finding the right, meaningful career. Whether early in your professional life, or at a critical mid-life gut-check, this book will help remind you how and why you can make a difference."

—DAVID MINIFIE, CHIEF EXPERIENCE OFFICER, CENTENE, AND FORMER ASSOCIATE MARKETING DIRECTOR, PROCTER & GAMBLE

IGNITE YOUR CAREER!

IGNITE
YOUR
CAREER!

Strategies and Tactics to
Unleash Your Potential

KRIS HOLMES

LIONCREST
PUBLISHING

IGNITE YOUR CAREER!
Strategies and Tactics to Unleash Your Potential

ISBN   978-1-5445-1449-9 *Hardcover*
       978-1-5445-1448-2 *Paperback*
       978-1-5445-1447-5 *Ebook*
       978-1-5445-1450-5 *Audiobook*

To Brian O'Connell.

Many thanks not only for being my mentor and trusted recruiter during my decade in marketing, but for having the faith to hire me remotely and to share your wisdom and guidance as I learned this magical craft. I love you and miss you!

CONTENTS

INTRODUCTION

"What do I want to do after I graduate college?"

Most students find themselves wondering about this sooner or later. Perhaps you already know the answer. If you do, that's great: I can help you achieve your goals. But if you don't, don't worry. You're not alone. In fact, you're one of the many.

Your friends might say they already know they're going to be lawyers or accountants or doctors, but that doesn't mean they've actually thought their careers through thoroughly. Some of them have never stopped to ask themselves, *What do I want to do for a career?* They may just be following their family legacy—expectations that may come back to bite them down the road.

To figure out where you will be most successful, you need to start with a different question: *What am I really good at and how can I leverage my strengths?*

This is one of the most important questions you can ask yourself at virtually any time in your career—but especially at the beginning.

In this book I can help you answer that question. I'll show you how to figure out your strengths and where they might lead. I'll also provide you with the tools to help you achieve your goals.

I've developed these tools during a twenty-five-year career as an executive recruiter. During that time, I've not only placed over 1,000 candidates in new jobs, I've counseled more than 20,000 others at all stages in their careers, including when they were just starting out. Whatever stage you're at, I can help you.

IT'S LIKE STEPPING OFF A CLIFF

If you're getting ready to graduate, you already know that it brings a lot of uncertainties. Throughout our entire education, we're taught to see graduation as a goal. Then you get there and it turns out to be just the starting point of another journey.

And there usually aren't many signposts.

Everything you've done up until now has been the next step on a journey that's likely been mapped out for you, from grade school through college. But now there are no more neatly laid-out steps to follow. As many universities note, "For most students, graduation is like stepping off a cliff."

There are so many potential career opportunities, which means that while this should be an exciting time, it's all so unknown and overwhelming that it can be completely debilitating. Almost two million young adults graduate from US colleges every year, and 30 to 40 percent wind up being underutilized in their careers. They take jobs that don't fully use their skills and intelligence. Not because they lack ability or talent, but because they don't know where they want to go or how to get there.

I don't want this to happen to you!

So here you are in college. You're surrounded by people who all seem as though they know what they're doing and where they want to go. Meanwhile, you're full of doubts. You're not sure what you want to do for a career. Looking toward the future might even make you feel like a bit of a fraud, as though someone's going to tap you on the shoulder and say, "What makes you believe you're in any position to start thinking about setting career goals?" Even if you know what you want to do, you may not know how to get started.

The truth is that many of your classmates feel the same way. Trust me, you are absolutely ready to lay the foundation for what happens next.

WHAT YOU'LL LEARN

This book will help you get started with easily relatable, practical advice for finding your career path. On these pages you'll find what you need most to be successful on your journey, beginning with self-evaluation, planning, and hard work.

In part I, we'll cover the strategic foundation for your career. Here's what you'll learn:

Chapter 1: Your Superpowers: I'll show you how to uncover your strengths and figure out how to leverage them in your job.

Chapter 2: Learn, Do, Leverage: I'll walk you through the phases of your career and what is critical in each phase.

Chapter 3: The Right Fit: I will explain how to assess company culture so that not only will you excel in a job, you'll also feel comfortable where you work. I strongly believe that culture and fit are crucial for happiness and satisfaction.

Chapter 4: The Long View: You'll learn how to keep your

eyes focused on your long-term goals and assess future opportunities, looking through a long-term lens to make sure you make smart career choices.

In part II, I'll take you through the practical tools needed to achieve your goals:

Chapter 5: A Winning Resume: How to write a resume that differentiates you, makes you appealing to employers, and sets you up for productive interviews.

Chapter 6: Build Your Networking Muscle: Why networking is so important and how to network effectively.

Chapter 7: Boosting the Odds: How to effectively apply for jobs.

Chapter 8: The Interview: How to prepare for interviews so *you* get to decide, "Do I want the job?"

Chapter 9: Win–Win Negotiation: How to negotiate a salary and benefits package effectively and build credibility along the way without burning goodwill.

Chapter 10: Resigning: It's a Small World: How to resign or decline a job professionally so that you leave on good terms.

THERE'S ONE CATCH

There's a catch, however, and it's one of the most important lessons in this book.

Here it is: There are no easy wins when you're searching for a job.

I can't do the work for you. You'll need to put in the effort, both to determine your goals and to build the tools to achieve them. It will take focus, time, and as I've already said, plenty of hard work. It will be worth it. I promise.

I am here to guide you every step of the way. Remember, you're investing in yourself—and the payback for your efforts will be enormous!

PART I

YOUR
STRATEGIC
FOUNDATION

CHAPTER 1

YOUR SUPERPOWERS

A critical step in determining your optimal career options is to figure out what I call your "strengths and superpowers."

Ask yourself, *"What are my innate strengths?"*

The only way to answer is to know yourself thoroughly. The better you understand yourself and can identify your strengths, the better you'll understand where you will thrive and succeed.

This will help you avoid two common traps when making career decisions:

1. False expectations
2. Fear of missing out

Early in their careers, many people choose certain jobs because they think they're supposed to. I know people who became lawyers or doctors or accountants because that's what their family did, but they were not happy in their careers. They let others' expectations influence their decisions.

Once they're on the "expectation boat," most people don't know how to get off. Even if the boat feels like it is sinking.

Fear of missing out (FOMO) is another real issue, especially in schools. FOMO can lead students to make decisions based on perception of credentials rather than what fits with their strengths (Christina Strong, who is a career coach at University of Michigan Business School, shared this concept with me).

These are several common failings:

- Students see what their friends are doing and start doubting themselves and their path.
- They see friends focusing on consulting, investment banking, and finance, careers that interview early and are perceived to be prestigious.
- When students watch people get jobs at top firms like Google, Amazon, P&G, or McKinsey Consulting, they question their own worth if they have offers at lesser-known companies.

- People focus on careers that appear to be lucrative but may not align with their strengths.

FIND THE RIGHT BOAT

I want to help you avoid getting on the wrong boat or being influenced by FOMO. I'm well placed to do that, because I made those mistakes myself.

Looking back, I now realize that I set out on the wrong boat at the start of my career. When I got onto the right boat thirteen years later, it changed my life.

Out of college, I was lucky enough to join a major department store in a training program to become a buyer. In my first year, I was assistant manager of a cosmetics department, which I loved. The next year I was supposed to become an assistant buyer who determines the assortment of goods to purchase. I decided it wasn't for me. Something didn't feel right.

I bailed.

Looking back, I am still shocked by what I did.

It took another two decades before I found out why I did it.

Back then, I explained my decision to human resources,

who suggested I shift into their department for the year. I loved HR, but I missed running a business, so I decided to go to business school at Kellogg. That took me into a new career in brand management and consumer marketing. I loved some aspects of my job, and I was really good at them, but there were still other parts that weren't as comfortable. They didn't come naturally.

I still didn't know why.

Fast-forward ten years and four companies. Suddenly, the company I was then working for was sold with no warning. I was out. While I was trying to figure out what to do next, I interviewed for marketing jobs and received offers to continue my career.

Then something came out of left field.

I was offered an opportunity by my favorite executive recruiter to go work for him.

Recruiting? It was a very different path from what I had been doing and what I was expected to do. I had gone to a top business school and I had spent ten years building my marketing capabilities. Few people thought I should switch boats. Although my husband was supportive, my family was frankly baffled that I would consider the move.

However, as I looked at the marketing director role that would be my next job in marketing, it made me very uncomfortable. I loved the brand manager job because so much of it was about dealing with people. The director role, while it was amazing, would have more politics and financials, profit and loss, and analytics—all the things I was not as good at and did not enjoy.

When the chance came along to try recruiting, I decided to make two lists of all the things I loved and hated about my previous jobs. I advise others to do the same thing when making decisions about their careers, and we'll explore this method later in the chapter.

Everything I liked kept coming back to people and relationships in the workplace: dealing with people, partnering with people, working as a team.

I realized that you couldn't find a more people-oriented role than recruiting. That's what the job *is*. You work with people every day. So, I made the change. I shifted into recruiting— and I fell into a career I loved. From day one, it felt right. It felt so natural it was almost easy. It fit so well with my strengths that I was very successful at it.

But I still didn't know why.

Then, a decade later, I finally had the aha moment.

My boss had his whole team read a book called *Discover Your Sales Strengths* by Benson Smith and Tony Rutigliano and take an online analysis called StrengthsFinder. On the test, my strengths showed up as:

· Winning others over (WOO)
· Communication
· Empathy
· Relator
· Connectedness
· Harmony

Not one was analytical.

As soon as I read the results, a lightbulb went off. *"That's why I'm good at recruiting."* All of my strengths are related to partnering and working with others. Finally, I could see why I had made my previous career decisions.

KNOW YOUR STRENGTHS

The concept behind this book is simple but powerful—and one I so believe in!

Figure out your strengths, find jobs that use them to the max, and you will be happy and successful.

I believe that corporate America has things backwards.

During performance reviews, companies often say, "Okay, you're great at these things." But then they move quickly on to, "Now let's talk about your weaknesses and focus on improving them."

Their focus should be on strengths, rather than weaknesses. Granted, some weaknesses are developmentally based, so once you are exposed to them you can convert them into strengths. But others are part of your DNA, and improving them is a no-win game. No matter how hard you work, that muscle will never develop.

My goal is to help you figure out your strengths and super-powers and leverage them so that you will be happy and successful *early on* in your career—not thirteen years down the road, like me.

A candidate of mine named Mia was in marketing for many years. She kept searching for the right place and fit. She initially picked consumer marketing, because fear of missing out told her it was the sexier side of marketing. But something always felt off. She was laid off numerous times. Eventually, she stepped back and got honest with herself. She made lists of her loves and hates, as I always suggest, and began to really think about her role.

It turned out that "influencing others," which is the abso-lute key to consumer marketing, was not a strength of hers at all. Instead, Mia realized that her superpowers were analysis and uncovering insights. This initially scared her to death. She felt as if she had wasted the last decade of her career. She almost wondered whether God had been sending her wake-up calls through her layoffs! But as she struggled through her self-doubt and FOMO, she figured out a path ahead. She shifted from consumer marketing into market research, which is much more data intensive. It played right to her strengths. She got promoted after one year, and she has become the person others go to when looking for data to support their ideas. Now she feels as though she is fully able to add value. "It feels really good to excel in my job and to be truly valued," she says.

GATHER INPUT

Knowing yourself sounds simple enough, but often external input is helpful. There are many opportunities to gather this information more quickly than Mia and I did, so that you start off with a core knowledge of your strengths from day one.

GET FEEDBACK

The first way is to talk to professors, coaches, or even family members. Ask them, "You know me. You've seen me in action, at school, on the field. What do you think are my strengths? What do you think I'm great at?"

If they come back and say, "You're incredibly analytical, you're great at solving problems, and you are really good at working independently," that might suggest you lean more toward science or some quantitative role. Or they might come back and say, "You have the gift of gab; you can talk to anybody any place. You have the innate ability to bring a team together and get everybody going in the same direction." If that's you, then working on your own will make you wilt and die. You probably have more aptitude to go into some sort of sales job or a role where you are going to end up influencing or managing large teams of people.

MAKE LISTS

A second way to try to assess strengths is by making lists, as I did when making my decision about recruiting, and as Mia did when reassessing her career. Take out two sheets of paper. On one, write down everything you have loved doing in current or past school or work roles; the things you enjoyed doing every single day. On the other piece of paper, write down what you hated doing. What are the things that make you miserable, that drive you crazy, that you're not as good at?

Put both lists away for a day, then take them back out and rank order each. Take the top five or ten off each list—the loves and the hates—and consolidate them into two shorter lists on a single sheet of paper. Always keep those shorter lists in front of you as you're looking for new jobs. It gives you focus. When you're looking at any new jobs, you want to have a lot more of the things you love than those you hate.

CAREER CENTER

A third way is to utilize your college or business school career center, or if you have already graduated, reach out to the alumni office. They may have tools and techniques to help you crystalize your strengths, and they can act as a sounding board. Having worked with thousands of students, they have great insight to share, as well as tools you can use.

TRUSTED RECRUITERS

A fourth way if you are out of school and into your career is to find trusted recruiters who are experts in your industry. They understand the nuances between different career paths and have partnered with thousands of others in your industry. If you share what you love doing and are good at, they may very well be able to map out the optimal direction for you to take moving forward. (I'll explain in chapter 7 how to find a reliable executive recruiter.)

ASSESSMENTS

A fifth and final way is something I strongly recommend to

everyone: Take impartial assessments, such as Strengths-Finder or YouScience, to learn more about yourself.

These are online tools you can use to figure out what you're good at so that you can focus on careers that will leverage your strengths. At the start of your career path, the range of choices can be overwhelming. An online assessment will help narrow the field, make it more manageable, and point you in the right direction. As YouScience explains: "Sooner or later we all figure it out. That 'aha' moment when we understand who we are, how we think, and what we should do with our lives—but what if we could do it sooner?"

StrengthsFinder

The more established of the two sites, StrengthsFinder, is part of the Gallup organization. It's an hour-long assessment consisting of a series of 177 paired statements. In each case, you choose which one best describes you, so you're giving your perception of yourself. The program measures your talents and your natural patterns of thinking, feeling, and behaving, and helps you figure out your strengths.

There are two versions of StrengthsFinder. The longer one comes up with thirty-four strengths, but early in your career it can be overwhelming and it's not necessary. Try the simpler version, which lists your five strengths with descriptors and suggestions about how your mix of strengths could be leveraged. It recognizes core strengths, such as executing, influencing, relationship building, and strategic thinking, and recommends possible roles. One such role is achiever, a person who is really good at executing things and could be a strong project manager. Another role is activator, somebody who is really good at influencing.

You can find StrengthsFinder at www.gallup.com/clifton strengths/en/253850/cliftonstrengths-for-individuals.aspx.

YouScience

YouScience is a more science-based assessment. Rather than asking about your perception of your strengths, it analyzes your hardwired potential by having you play a series of nine, short, psychometric games on the computer. Your gameplay and results allow the program to figure out how your brain works, and what your natural aptitude, talents, and strengths are. It then gives you an enormous number of options of careers where these strengths could be leveraged. Their website is https://www.youscience. com, and if you use this code, IGNITE20, you will receive a discount.

YouScience works with many colleges and high schools. The Senior VP Marketing & Sales at the company told me he saw the power of the assessment personally when he had both of his children take it.

His daughter's mix of aptitudes and interests suggested veterinarian. She thought, "Yes, I love dogs and animals, and I have an aptitude for science and engineering. It would be exciting to go into this field."

The site helped her blend her natural talents and interests to uncover something she's now passionate about. Rather than being overwhelmed about applying to schools and not knowing where to start, she could focus on, "What do I have to do to become a veterinarian? What classes do I take? Where are the best veterinarian programs?" She then started her journey in high school by choosing to take an anatomy and physiology class instead of the more popular— and easier—psychology course all her friends took.

When the VP's son took the assessment, the top-fit careers he matched to were construction manager and anesthe-siologist, two very different paths. Because he was able to understand how his natural abilities translated across both careers, however, he was able to focus his explora-tion in these two areas instead of aimlessly considering the thousands of other possibilities out there. Rather than be overwhelmed by applying to all the schools his friends were looking at, he was able to be more focused on finding out which colleges had the best programs for construction management or pre-med.

After a few school visits and conversations with people in

his two respective career paths, he realized that what he was most passionate about was helping people. Being able to incorporate his passions with his talents led him to focus on pre-med.

WHAT'S YOUR BULLSEYE?

Armed with the insight you get from StrengthsFinder or YouScience, there are still many different paths you could take. You will likely not find the perfect fit initially. No one ends up in their dream job straight out of college. Or very few. Today, a tiny percentage of people go to a company and stay there for their entire career. Most have somewhere between nine and eleven jobs after they get out of college, and that number is growing. Some of those jobs may involve people moving within their current company, but many of those jobs are going to take them to new companies.

Every role you take will allow you to figure out a little more about what you want to do. For each one, ask yourself, "What do I like about it? What don't I like?" This will help you figure out the bullseye you're aiming for, and how to continue to tighten your aim. If you start by taking one of the online assessments, you may start out by hitting two or three rings out from your bullseye rather than being completely off target.

With people living longer, and staying healthier longer,

a new graduate might have forty, fifty, or more years to work. You could spend that time constantly climbing uphill because your job doesn't fit with your strengths. Or you could be in a job that feels as natural as breathing because it's leveraging what you're innately good at.

Think of it like that, and the decision is easy.

If you start with an accurate picture of your strengths, you will save yourself a world of hurt. You can avoid banging your head against the wall trying to move a weakness needle that has little upside. In addition, doing research and taking an assessment may actually give you the language to explain why you're not getting on someone else's expectation boat.

It could help you tell your family: "You know what? My strengths lie in a different place. I'm wired differently. While I'm so proud you guys are all doctors (or whatever), I'm really good at collaboration and empathy, and I have an ability to bring people along and influence them. I think I can leverage my strengths in sales, and while you may think that salesperson is a four-letter word, I'm going to knock it out of the park."

I'll conclude this chapter with the thoughts of one of my associates, Dominic Iacono, who is now managing director of a Fortune 50 company in Hong Kong. As the manager of a large team, he thinks a lot about finding people's strengths as a way to achieve his own and his teams' goals.

Dominic read an article on LinkedIn about the rapper Dr. Dre, who was quoted as saying, "My greatest talent is knowing exactly what I want to hear."

Dominic told me, "That got me to thinking. I reflected on what my greatest talent is, or whether I have any talent at all. What is it that I actually bring to the people in the teams I've worked on?"

He decided that he only had one overriding skill. His superpower is developing people.

"I think my ability to assess people's specific talent and potential is high. It's the only way I've been successful throughout my military and civilian career. I've really surrounded myself with talented people, recognizing what each individual's unique brilliance is, and trying my best to put them in positions that bring out those qualities where their talents can make an impact on winning."

He continued, "Why focus people on things they're not as good at? Wouldn't it be better to focus on and leverage the things they're good at, and then get them enrolled where they can unleash their talent? Wouldn't people enjoy their work more and feel good about what they contribute when they're getting praise for doing a good job on something they excel at?"

As I shared earlier, the StrengthsFinder assessment showed me my strengths. But what is my superpower?

I found out that it's WOO—winning others over. I simply love meeting new people and winning them over. WOO is the cornerstone of my success as an executive recruiter. It is what allows me to connect with people immediately over the phone and build trust, and it serves as the foundation for our long-term relationship.

In summary, spending the time to figure out what you are really good at will allow you to factor your strengths into your career planning and set you up for a productive and successful career journey.

I encourage you to take some time to log onto and explore the self-assessment tools StrengthsFinder and/or You-Science. You'll then be better equipped to learn about the three phases of your career in chapter 2.

CHAPTER 2

LEARN, DO, LEVERAGE

Hopefully, you've tapped into Strengthsfinder or You-Science, and you've done a deep self-assessment. You've figured out what you're good at, what your strengths are, and what your superpowers might be. You've gained more of an idea about where you might want to take your career.

Armed with that information, it's time to look forward. In this chapter, I'll explain the different career phases you'll go through.

THREE PHASES

There are three phases in your career that apply to whatever industry or field you are in.

These phases are:

1. Learn
2. Do
3. Leverage

LEARN

The *learn* phase usually comes in the earlier part of your career, when you're building your foundational skills. At this stage everything you're doing, or at least most of it, is new and unfamiliar.

If you shift to a new career at a later point, you will return at least in part to the learn phase. Consider the example of a lawyer who decides he no longer wants to practice law and instead wants to move into marketing. While he will already have gone through the learn phase as a lawyer, he is now entering a completely new field, so he will return to the learn phase of his second career.

At the learn stage, you are gaining knowledge and experience. You're building your skillset in your chosen field. Your goal is to learn as many relevant skills as possible, and to become an expert at them. How do you do this? One of the most effective ways is to work for strong companies in your industry, or the best you can attain. You should aim to work for knowledgeable experts, who can train you in the best practices for the skills you need. In this way, you're not just learning; you're learning the gold standard. This will allow you to keep more options open down the road and set you up to achieve your long-term goals.

This is the investment phase of your career: you and the organization are both investing time, money, and resources to help you build your capabilities. The stronger the career foundation you create now, the higher you can build your career.

Think about this analogy:

Each time you build a new skill, you create a new tool for your toolbox. Your goal is to fill your toolbox with quality tools, so that eventually you have enough that you can go build something special.

Be warned: the learn phase is not easy. I'm a huge believer in the idea that the first time you do almost anything, it's hard. It's like climbing a mountain without walking poles and a clearly marked path. Each time you learn or use a skill, you are gathering the equipment you need to create a path up the mountain. Each time you climb it gets easier and easier. By the tenth time you use a skill, you've got it. You know your stuff. By now you're running up the mountain because you have carved a path, you have good footing, and you're sure of the way. That's the goal of the learning phase: building a quality skillset that will enable you to shift to the next phase of your career.

DO

In the *doing* phase, you apply the knowledge and skills you've learned to deliver results in your field and to generate a strong track record of success. This often involves being promoted to a new role. In the marketing world, for example, people in the learning phase might be an assistant or associate brand manager working for somebody who directs and oversees their work. In the doing phase, they'll be promoted to fill that brand manager position themselves. They'll work much more autonomously, both setting strategies and developing plans to achieve their goals.

In the doing phase, you know both what to do and how to do it. You have more experience, autonomy, and authority, so you can take the ball and run with it. You neither want nor need somebody micromanaging you and looking over your shoulder.

To return to the toolbox analogy:

Your toolbox is now full of strong, quality tools. Now you can take the toolbox and go build a quality house.

In the doing phase of your career, you're taking the skills you have honed and using them to build something. In this phase, you will build over and over, and you will have both successes and failures. Whenever you trip or fall, the key is to recognize your mistake and figure out why you made it. Then you can course-correct, so you won't make the same mistake again. That is how home builders continue to improve the quality of the houses they create.

The doing phase is all about becoming an expert in your field. You have to "*do*" multiple times. This might be in different types of businesses or under different scenarios, or it could be a whole variety of things in your specific industry. The key thing is that you need to do over and over until you are an expert in doing.

In terms of our house-building analogy, being expert means that you don't only know how to build one type of house. During your phase of doing, you build high-quality homes with many different architectural designs.

At this point in your career, you are adding value and the company is getting their return on investment and hopefully rewarding you for it. During this phase, you should look for opportunities to begin leading through mentorship, leading corporate initiatives, or managing others. Working for a top company in your industry is not as critical now as it was before, because you have developed your capabilities and are putting them to good use. You might decide to move to a midsized organization where you have more chance to truly make an impact.

LEVERAGE

When you get to the point when you're ready to have more influence, you've reached the third stage of your career: *leverage*. This is when you take the knowledge and experience you have gained and move your business ahead by leading a team. In other words, you show that you have the ability to get things done through others. In the leverage phase, you are teaching people and working with them to guide them through their own learning and doing phases. You're an expert in your field, and you also have the knowledge and passion to teach others how to succeed.

Leveraging needs a very different skillset from doing or learning. Many people trip up at this phase, because they've never been taught how to manage people well. Often, they're so used to "doing" things themselves, they can't let go. Being a strong leader and manager does not come naturally to everybody. I recommend that people reach out and seek help from mentors or attend seminars and classes to learn how to both manage and leverage effectively. If you want to be successful in your career, you need to excel in these areas.

Knowing how to set your people up for success will allow you to deliver exceptional results as well as build world-class talent. However, some people choose to focus on more knowledge leverage, rather than people leverage. They add value by becoming the absolute guru in their area of expertise. This type of leverage has enormous value too.

In the leveraging phase, you might decide to move to an even smaller company where you can help build its organizational capabilities. At this point in your career this makes intrinsic sense. You know what to do and how to do it, and you are ready to teach others best practices.

In summary, going back to our toolbox analogy:

- At the *learn* stage, you are developing your tools.
- At the *do* stage, you are taking your toolbox and building quality houses.
- At the *leverage* stage, you're now the general contractor. You're directing people who are building quality houses with their own toolboxes.

Now you're familiar with the three stages of your career, it's time to consider where you'll have the best opportunity to learn, do, and leverage with maximum impact. To understand that, the next chapter looks at company culture and what's the right fit for you.

CHAPTER 3

THE RIGHT FIT

So, you've graduated from college or graduate school, and you've got the job you wanted at the company you wanted to work for. You've been building your skills in the learning phase but you're not happy. In fact, you're downright miserable. What are you doing wrong?

The answer is, probably nothing. Many times, the person is not the problem. Nor is the company. The problem is how the two fit together.

If an individual doesn't fit with the culture of a company, everything becomes a struggle. It all feels off.

I remember a candidate who was a few years out of business school. She had a very good job and was learning loads, but she was miserable. She told me, "Every day, on the way to work, I have to pull over to the side of the road and cry. That's what I have to do to make it through the day." Another candidate told me, "I pray for red lights on my way to work to put off the pain as long as possible!"

A third candidate who I worked with was a couple of years out of school and, again, was absolutely miserable. He had gained twenty pounds. He didn't feel right in his own skin, and not just because of the weight he had put on. He had always been an optimist, but he suddenly found himself being pessimistic about everything. He felt as if there were a dark cloud above his head.

As we talked about why he wasn't comfortable where he worked, it became clear that the job was not the problem. He loved the job, and it fit the career path he had mapped out for himself.

The problem was the company's values. How they operated did not align with his own values and style.

Together, we found a company with a culture that fit his, and he moved there. The change was remarkable. He told me, "I feel like I fit. I feel like every day when I go to work, I'm welcomed. It is like going home. I have a bounce in my step and the world is good."

In addition, the weight fell off him. He didn't even have to try to lose it. He was back in a state of physical and mental health.

Now, he could have thrown the baby out with the bath water. He could have blamed his unhappiness on the job and given up on his career ambition. But what he discovered was that he loved his job. He just didn't love where he was doing it.

The job wasn't the problem. The company wasn't the problem. A bad culture fit was the problem.

CONTRAST OF CULTURES

What is culture fit? Culture fit is how closely the norms and values of a company align with those of an employee. Unlike hard skills, culture fit cannot be taught. Lack of culture fit is damaging for both sides. For the individual, it can lead to unhappiness, low self-worth, and poor mental health. For the company, it can lead to poor productivity, excessive absence, and high turnover of staff.

Research has shown that almost 50 percent of job satisfaction is due to an employee's fit with a company's culture.

There are many different types of company cultures. I believe strongly that there are no good or bad cultures. There are only good or bad fits.

Trying to fit into a culture that does not naturally fit you makes everything tougher. It takes a huge amount of energy to pretend to be someone you are not!

Cultures can be polarizing. On one hand, some companies are very collaborative. They are so inclusive that everyone must approve things before you can move forward. On the other hand is an extremely fast-paced, action-oriented company culture, where how you get things done is often less important than simply getting them done. These companies often believe in failing and learning fast, so they make decisions very quickly.

Depending on your personality, you might thrive in a particular culture—or you might struggle.

How comfortable are you with ambiguity? Do you prefer more autonomy, or do you like having a playbook? Are you a conformist or a nonconformist? A rule follower or somebody who likes to push the envelope? How does the company react to what you do? Do they celebrate people who push for change, or do they want to do things just as they've always done them?

Companies know how critical culture fit is to set employees up for success. They have seen the best and brightest hires fail miserably due to lack of culture fit. As a result, they often overlook gaps in skills in order to recruit a person who "fits" their organization. Many skills can be trained and taught. Fit cannot.

Who you work for can impact how much you enjoy your job, so when you are interviewing for a role be mindful of who your boss would be. Consider whether you actually like them. What is their style managing others, and what do their subordinates think of them? Is their style indicative of the company's culture? Having said this, never take a job because you want to work with a specific manager. You have no control as to whether they will move to another role or even leave the company.

Some people tend to focus on being passionate about things such as a company's category or the benefits the company offers. While I understand the desire to feel connected to the company or to have key benefits, I do not believe you should seek out those things at the expense of building the right skills to achieve your long-term goals.

In the learning phase of your career, stay focused on building skills and expertise. This will help you get the job of your dreams down the road.

ASSESSING CULTURE

It's one thing to tell you to assess the culture fit any time you are searching for a new role. It's another thing to do it. Assessing fit well does not always come naturally. It's a learned skill, and sometimes you have to "kiss a few frogs before you find your prince."

There are ways to get a sense for a company's culture. Here are a few questions and suggestions to help:

- Go to the company website and read their values. Do they resonate with you?
- Do the employees' behaviors match the company's stated values?
- When you are interviewing, pay attention to how people interact with each other. Are they friendly or are they more serious or reserved?
- Are people in the office smiling? Do they seem happy?
- When you ask people why they love the company, what do they talk about?
- If you get an offer, ask to talk to some peers and probe them on culture.
- Ask about the office layout. Do people have offices or cubicles, or is it an open plan? Whichever it is, do they like it?
- Is the office chaotic, lively, or serene?
- If you know anyone who presently works for the company or has worked for them in the past, reach out for their perspective on the organization.
- Review the company on sites such as Glassdoor, but take whatever you read with a grain of salt. The employ-

ees who post on such sites are typically those who either really love or really hate the company or culture. Most people are in between.

· Did your time inside the company during your interview make you feel energized and excited or uncomfortable?

No matter how much information you gather, culture fit is still sometimes difficult to assess. This is when I believe you need to listen to your gut instinct, the combination of your heart and head. The discomfort you feel about the company might just be nerves, which is normal. If there is something else nagging at you, however, don't ignore it. Try to figure out what it is.

Whenever I, or others in my family, have made bad decisions, it has usually been when we haven't figured things out. There's been a little voice raising objections inside our heads, but we haven't listened. Those are the decisions you often come to regret.

A great way to think about culture is like a science experiment:

· A bad culture is toxic and kills.
· A neutral culture is where you can survive but not thrive.
· A positive culture is one where you flourish.

Being mindful of a company's culture and how it aligns

with your personality will help you avoid land mines. Don't jump at an offer because it has more money, a better title, or ideal geography without also assessing the culture fit.

Remember: There are no good or bad cultures—but there absolutely *are* good and bad culture fits. That's something to keep in mind as we move on to chapter 4, which explains why it's so critical to keep your eyes on the long view.

CHAPTER 4

THE LONG VIEW

Years ago, I was working at Kraft Foods. I loved it, but at a certain point I was offered two different manager roles. One of them fit me perfectly. It leveraged my strengths, and it built on something I had done in my last job that I loved. The other job was pretty alien and uncomfortable for me, but it had a higher base and a higher bonus, and so I took it.

Looking back, it was the worst career move I ever made.

I wish I had a do-over. It's not that I didn't learn a lot, because I did. But it was a grind. It called for skills I hadn't developed and that weren't in my wheelhouse. It did not align with my strengths, and it did nothing to progress my career toward my desired goals.

I realized this very soon after taking the job, but by then I was locked in. I had signed up for a tour of duty, and I had to complete it.

The reason I'm telling you this story is to underline the importance of keeping your eyes on the long term. Career choices are not just about what you're doing today, or even tomorrow. They're about building your skills and experiences so that you can figure out and ultimately achieve your long-term goals—and those goals will likely evolve over time.

The key is to continue to learn and grow while continuing to keep options open as you progress your career.

As we saw in chapter 2, the learning phase of your career is all about getting experience and building your skills and capabilities. As you progress, opportunities will come up. They might involve an internal promotion, or moving to a new company. When any opportunity does arise, don't just consider the immediate benefits. Assess it against the backdrop of your long-term goals.

That's where I went wrong. I took the wrong step for the wrong reasons: short-term rewards, a little more money, and a higher bonus.

VISUALIZE YOUR CAREER

I use a number of analogies to help candidates keep their eyes on their long-term career.

First, always remember: *Your career is a marathon, not a sprint.*

It doesn't matter how fast you're running if you're on the wrong track.

YOUR CAREER TREE

A second analogy I often use to help candidates visualize the long term is logical and easy to remember. My candidates tell me, ten or fifteen years later, that they still use it when they're making decisions.

Think about your career like a tree:

- Your education and credentials are your roots.
- Your early career experience is building your trunk. Early in their careers, everyone has a wobbly little tree. But as you build your experience, that trunk gets stronger and bigger and you move up.
- Your goal is to get high up on the trunk before you branch out.

Next time you go outside, look at a tree. There are usually

a couple of wispy branches low down, but they're not very long. They don't go anywhere, and they're isolated. They don't overlap with any other branches. Tree experts call them "suckers."

Higher up the trunk, there are far more branches. There's a lot of overlap with other branches and even with other trees.

When you branch out from a position higher up your trunk, not only are there more opportunities to explore, but there are also more opportunities to move from branch to branch.

Beware of branching out too early.

I sometimes hear candidates say something like, "I've had two years' experience in consumer marketing at a strong training company, and I'm thinking of shifting into apparel (or technology, or e-commerce, etc.)."

In marketing, after two years of experience, you're absolutely still in the learning phase.

I share the tree analogy, and I tell them:

> "You're trying to branch out very early on in your career. This branch might work out and your long-term career could be purely in apparel, or technology, or e-commerce, which is okay. But if it doesn't pan out, you'll have no choice but to

come back to where you left two years ago and start building again, which often means at a lesser company or with a lower title and less money. Even if you are willing to do this, there are too many others who stayed put in consumer marketing and kept learning and built their trunk, making them less risky hires."

Think of someone further on in their career, higher up the tree. They might be a brand manager, so they have five or six years of experience. In terms of *learn, do, leverage*, they're in the "doing" phase. They've run a couple of businesses and proved that they can utilize the skills they have developed to build a brand and deliver success.

If this candidate wants to branch out to apparel, or e-commerce, or technology, it's a fine strategic move. They have a sturdy trunk, which is a great foundation nobody can take away.

This time, if the new branch doesn't work, they can return to their trunk and still have many other branches they can move to where their blend of experiences will serve them well. They're high up on the trunk where branches overlap, and it's far easier to move from one to another.

Do remember, if something feels very wrong and you decide you're on the wrong tree, it's always possible to change, as we saw with Mia in chapter 1. When people go back to school or change their careers completely, as I did, or move from lawyer to marketer as we discussed previously, it is like building a new tree.

Over twenty-five years in recruiting, I have seen many people make bad moves. They are swayed by money or a title or perceived short-term gains. It's critical to keep focused on building your skills and keeping your long-term goals in mind.

Every time you make a career decision, think of the tree.

BE A POOL SHARK

A third analogy I often share with candidates is to *think about your career as a game of pool.* Sometimes, it's really tempting to take the easy shot in the corner pocket. But a pool shark knows that it's more important to line up the other balls to win the game. It's not about the single shot. Instead, it's about setting up the series of successful shots that will ultimately lead to sinking the black and winning the game.

A job with more money or a better title is like the easy shot. You make the shot, but you're left in a poor position for your next shot and you reduce your chances of winning the game.

When you think about career moves and opportunities,

think about lining up your next two shots: "How does this move set me up for my next two moves to get me where I want to go?"

EGO IS YOUR ENEMY

Whenever you consider career choices, there's one key thing to remember: *Don't let your ego make your decision for you.* Don't get tempted by the satisfaction of making the easy shot in the corner pocket if it could cost you the game.

I was recently talking to a candidate who was an associate at a top-credential training company. He got an offer at the director level at a much smaller company. That's a two-level promotion. He thought, "They see my value. This move is going to accelerate my career far beyond my peers. It's so cool." He was proud to jump two levels. He listened to his ego and took the job.

Six months later, he told me "Oh, man, that was a bad decision."

In that time, he had realized that his new company didn't value marketing. He also saw that he didn't yet have the skillset for the job. He was still in the learning phase of his career, but he was trying to jump into a leveraging phase. He was still missing many of the tools he needed. On top of that, there was nobody at the new company for him to learn from. Not only that. In other companies, everyone knew the title was inflated. The marketplace is savvy. It understands what experience counts and what doesn't.

As you build your career, aim always to work with and for smart people who have more experience than you do: that is how you learn and grow. In the learning phase of your career, you do not want to be the person who has the highest level of expertise in your field. That's the danger of the easy shot.

The candidate who took the easy shot is now losing the game. The job felt good and it stroked his ego, but it was a bad long-term strategic move. He lost leverage. He had to go back to where he was to get back on track again—if he even can. Now there's a yellow flag up beside his name because future employers are going to look at his move and question his decision-making skills. He will be competing against others with the same title who have far better experience.

That is never a good place to be.

GETTING CARRIED AWAY

There are many reasons people move jobs. Companies get sold, spouses get a new job, a family member gets ill. Sometimes it's out of our control. If you can explain it, you can take the issue off the table. But oftentimes, if somebody has moved a lot, the perception is they're not strong at their role or have poor decision-making abilities.

This happened to one of my peers at Kraft. After about two years, she left to go to a smaller company with a bigger title. She quickly realized her mistake.

The way she explained her decision stuck with me. "It was like I was on a highway and came up to an exit with a lot of bright lights that looked really appealing. I got excited, and I exited that highway. And, literally, the minute I exited I knew that I should be back on that highway."

She came back to Kraft with her tail between her legs and said, "I made a bad decision. I'd like to come back." She did return—but again, that yellow flag was flying. The company now questioned her commitment and decision making. She had a big hill to climb to get her career back on track.

The smartest thing you can do to avoid bad career decisions is to keep going back to the framework of your long-term goals:

- Does this move keep me on the right track? Is it building the right skillset?
- Can I deliver strong success here?
- Is it setting me up for success in my next few jobs?

- Or is it just stroking my ego and giving me short-term gains that in the long term will be painful?

Don't let ego cloud your judgment. Smart, steady, long-term focus is what wins the career race.

Keep your focus on the long term by keeping these analogies and visuals at the front of your mind:

- Your career is a marathon, not a sprint.
- Your career is like a tree.
- Think of your career as a game of pool.

Be mindful of these three analogies as part of the strategic foundation of your career, together with the other principles we've reviewed in part I: figuring out your strengths, understanding the different phases of learn, do, and leverage, and identifying what culture fits you best. These are principles that can guide your whole career. In part II, I'll share with you the practical tools you need to put them into action to apply for—and get!—the jobs you want.

PART II

PRACTICAL TOOLS

CHAPTER 5

A WINNING RESUME

Your resume is a vital tool in your job search. Don't try to be fancy. Make it clear, easy to digest, consistent, and compelling.

A winning resume is an important marketing tool that serves three purposes:

1. It gets you noticed and, hopefully, pulls you out of the mass of resumes.
2. If it's a great resume, it will prompt an invitation to interview.
3. It will help structure the interview.

Your resume is yours. It's your chance to help the reader understand who you are, what you've done and accomplished, and what you may be capable of achieving in the future. Very importantly, it helps you build your story in preparation for your job search and interviewing.

GETTING NOTICED

The person reading your resume is busy and does not want to waste time during the search process. They're focused on finding the right person to fill the role, so they are going to look for relevant information quickly.

With a typical resume, if you get an eight-second first glance, you're doing well. The easier you make it for the reader to glean the salient points, recognize what you've accomplished, and understand your strong progression, the more likely you are to get to the interview stage.

I often get asked how long a resume should be. It really differs, depending on how much experience you have. Out of college or graduate school, a one-page resume is appropriate as it gives you enough space to speak to your experiences. Once you have more experience, two pages is the norm.

LAYING OUT YOUR RESUME

Like a news article, resumes are read on two levels: headline, then body copy. The headline gives the reader a snapshot of the information they need in order to decide whether they should invest the time to read the rest of your resume. The headlines are your education, the companies you have worked for, your titles, and, at the doing and leveraging phases, your responsibilities. The body copy is what you did and what your results were.

What goes at the top of your resume is what you are telling a prospective employer is the number-one reason they should want to hire you. When you are coming out of college, graduate school, or law school, your education goes first, along with your extracurricular activities, your leadership positions, and possibly your GPA (if strong). At this stage, the recent completion of your degree is why they are looking to hire you. Once you begin your career, your relevant experience becomes the number-one reason they would have interest in recruiting you. Your education is still relevant, but it is no longer the primary driver for their interest in your resume.

List your experience in reverse chronological order, as the most recent experience will be of the most interest to potential employers.

While relevant content is very important, pay attention to the layout of your resume. You want to make it as easy to read as possible.

Here are the basics:

- Use a consistent typeface, with bold and capital headings for the different sections.
- Have enough white space so it's easy to read. Don't cram it in by making the typeface too small. I like 10.5 or 11 pt.
- There are two formats that are acceptable, dates on the left or the right. Whichever you choose, have a consistent location for dates and geography.
- Bullet points versus paragraphs:
  - Paragraphs take more effort to read, and you're asking the reader to invest time to digest them.
  - Bullet points are bite size, and therefore much easier for the reader to understand what you're trying to convey.
- If you have a bullet point that has sub-segments, it's fine to use indented bullet points underneath an umbrella bullet (see above).
- Use action-oriented language. Choose words like "lead," "create," "develop," or "initiate" versus something like "participated in," which is passive.
- At the doing and leveraging phases, have a one-sentence description under your title stating what you are or were responsible for in that role.
- Cover the breadth of your responsibilities, and have language that indicates analytical strength or in-depth knowledge.
- Most importantly, where you have them add in your accomplishments and successes.

Do not include a photograph or odd columns. Trust me: In the world of resume writing, odd is not a good thing.

WHAT GOES IN YOUR RESUME

The actual content of your resume may vary, depending on the phases of your career.

Coming out of school, you're in the learning phase of your career, as we discussed in chapter 2. At this stage, an interviewer will be evaluating the depth of your training, the breadth of your learning, and your relevant results. In the learning phase, they want to know what boxes you have checked. If you have accomplishments, they are the icing on the cake—the key is whether you've developed relevant skills.

Under your education, include any leadership or significant service positions, bulleted out. This will show leadership, initiative, and potentially strong project management skills.

Then add any work experience, such as internships. Here, potential employers are seeking evidence of intelligence, leadership, initiative, project management, creativity, ability to work with others, and analytical skills.

Of course, every profession is different in terms of the exact skills and experiences you will speak to.

SUSAN STREET
Colorado Springs, Colorado
SStreet@coloradocollege.edu (504) 399-2324

EDUCATION
STATE COLLEGE, Colorado Springs, CO   8/2017- Present
Candidate for Bachelor of Arts degree, History Major, Class of '21
- Current GPA: 3.23
- Dean's List last two semesters
- Member of the Club Ultimate Frisby Team
- Executive Board–College Volunteers Organization
- Member of Women's A Capella Group
- Mentor to at risk youth

WORK EXPERIENCE
UNIQUE HOMES, New Orleans, LA   Summer 2019
Leading designer and dealer of prefabricated homes
Marketing Intern
- Developed reports to assess website and integrated marketing performance using Google Analytics
- Managed the company's presence at the Dwell on Design conference
  - Coordinated efforts to ensure timelines were met
  - Trained office personnel on lead retrieval software
  - Fielded questions from and sold homes to over 5,000 potential clients over a three-day convention
- Researched and compiled reports on opportunity for market expansion into vertical spaces
- Created award submission for the 2019 Builder's Choice and Custom Home Design Awards including project statements, photographs, and project specifications
- Initiated and orchestrated office reorganization that had been delayed for three years
- Designed brochures and reports to send to clients and potential leads

NEW ORLEANS TOURISM OFFICE, New Orleans, LA   Summer 2018
Intern
- College Grant Recipient
- Organized the inaugural Tourism Symposium for NOLA
  - Recruited event participants and speakers from across the Tourism industry
  - Created advertising materials, assisted in creating webpage, contacted newspapers, radio stations, and other news outlets to market the event
  - Planned and managed logistics the day of the event
- Developed the Governmental Framework and began contacting key groups to gain commitments
- Summarized the findings of the Event into an easy-to-read document and created a multilayered map of the results
- Authored an article on New Orleans Times-Picayune e-Newsletter
- Collected Tourism-oriented information and created a tab on the NOLA Government webpage

FRANKLIN ROOSEVELT DAY CAMP, New Orleans, LA   Summer 2013-2017
Camp Counselor

INTERESTS
Marathon runner and on board of local Big Brothers Big Sisters NOLA chapter

This is an example of a college student resume.

In the "doing" phase of your career, an employer will again be evaluating your breadth of responsibilities, but they also will be looking more in depth for accomplishments. If you remember, this is the phase when you're taking that toolbox you've put together and you're building. So now, they're evaluating what you have built and the results you delivered. You need to really assess how you positively impacted the projects you worked on. This is not the time to be self-effacing.

If you've worked at companies that few people have heard of, or your industry is unique, add a one-sentence description of the company underneath its name. While you might think an employer would look up the company for themselves, they neither have the time nor desire to do so. Putting it on your resume provides insight into the company and what they do.

Prospective employers also want to see evidence of progression. Progression at your organization could be a promotion, a rotation, or additional responsibilities. All of these show you are doing a good job.

At the leveraging phase, potential employers are going to be evaluating accomplishments and your ability to lead and leverage your expertise and track record to deliver results, not just on your business, but on a group of businesses or at the overall corporate level.

JOHN SMITH

City, State, Zip
Personal Phone Number • Email

EXPERIENCE

8/2017–Present ENTREPRENEURIAL "LEVERAGING" COMPANY　　　　　　　　International
Senior Vice President

Lead overseas division with full P&L responsibility and develop it into one of the company's top growth markets with significant investment and management attention.

- 20XX: Net Sales +21% and Margin +25% on $107mm base.
- Moved from #2 in share for Premium Category to #1 on fundamentals and moved from #3 in Adult to #1 on a highly successful relaunch. On track for $XXMM+ in 20XX.
- Design and manage organization of 165 direct employees and 200+ contractors
- Design distribution strategy and manage 9 wholesalers and distributors

4/2010–8/2017 MID-SIZED "DOING/LEVERAGING" COMPANY　　　　　　　Various
1/2015–8/2017 Vice President　　　　　　　　　　　　　　　　　　International

Leader of company's 100+ employee business with full P&L responsibility and $XXMM in budget. Skills P&L management, team building, ecommerce, digital, CRM, distribution design, managing across cultures.

- Successfully turned around a developing market business: Gross margin +11pts, Yr 1 & 2 sales +4% and +10%, returns -40%.
- Implemented new forecasting system, changed distributors, restructured sales, and replaced Nielsen with internal data system with greater coverage and accuracy.
- Developed leadership teams, all now considered top talent and promotable.

7/2013–12/2014 Director　　　　　　　　　　　　　　　　　　　　New York, NY

Operating lead for a team responsible for 8 brands. Grew portfolio +14% in a flat category with share gains in all product categories.

- Re-launched brand and grew category with company's first major media effort in the US. Campaign built and launched in 6 weeks; brand achieved 2x previous sales within 2 years.
- Leveraged differentiated claims on two brands to reignite growth in the channel. Both franchises achieved high single to low double-digit sales and share growth.
- Launched a new product in mid-2014 with >$25mn annual sales and currently growing >15% annually.
- Managed 6 direct reports and 3 agencies to deliver business objectives.

5/2010–7/2013 Senior Manager　　　　　　　　　　　　　　　　　　New York, NY

Led the Global Specialty Business Unit, a strategic marketing group charged with the regional expansion and innovation pipeline that represented ~15% of total company turnover.

- Expanded portfolio into emerging markets, with sales up +24% and projected value 1.5x – 2x previous base.
- Created and transferred to markets numerous consumer and professional tools to support portfolio growth, including digital content, core advertising, and medical sales capabilities.
- Built two category pipelines from scratch by identifying category experts within R&D, enrolling them in consumer need identification, and championing their innovations through stage gate processes.
- Led the evaluation and offer for a joint venture with a novel enterprise.
- Responsibility increased twice since taking role, ending in management of total group.

2/2000–5/2010 TOP TIER TRAINING COMPANY　　　　　　　　　　　Various
9/2008–5/2010 Senior Brand Manager　　　　　　　　　　　　　　Los Angeles, CA

Led the largest brand in company at $500mn and largest product in the world.

- Over delivered brand objective by +$50mn during the launch of store brand and 4 branded competitors.
- Directed $150Mn+ marketing budget across TV, print, internet, influencer, ER, ethnic, retail, and direct opportunities for maximum ROI. Resulted in the highest scoring advertising in brand history and among top 5% across company.
- Managed NFL and NASCAR sponsorships to 30+ weeks out-of-aisle merchandising in Retailer and other major channels. Created "Most Valuable" award and launched at major sporting event.
- Directed network of agencies focusing on major media, digital, sports marketing, trade marketing, PR.

6/2006–9/2008 <u>Customer Marketing Manager – Major Retailer</u>   Minneapolis, MN
               Managed all in and out-of-store marketing activities for the company's portfolio at major retailer, one of
               company's top 10 customers in the U.S. Ranked #1 by Retailer in marketing report - a 1st for company.
               • Consulted with Retailer on shopper centric approaches, especially shopper segmentation and targeting.
                 Successfully moved Retailer marketing to a shopper-based approach, a first in Retailer history and a
                 major win for the company.
               • Developed and executed customized in and out-of-store launch programs for top-tier products, earning
                 best-in-US recognition.

10/2004–6/2006 <u>Brand Manager</u>   San Francisco, CA
               Developed products for global launch including one joint venture and one specialty. Developed expertise in
               managing across a large company to a startup model.
               • Constructed story for product by working closely with patent holder to articulate method-of-action; work
                 ultimately became pre-marketing education plan.
               • Received 3rd set of Recognition Shares for strategy work done on joint venture.

3/2000–10/2004 <u>Assistant Brand Manager</u>   San Francisco, CA
               • Increased sales and share of brands through both consumer marketing efforts, including leading the
                 $60mn+ consumer launch of brand X, company's largest brand in the category.

1/1996 –9/1998 HEALTHCARE COMPANY   Los Angeles, CA
               <u>Territory Manager</u>
               • Surpassed sales goals to consistently be top 25% or better of region's representatives.

<u>EDUCATION</u>
TOP RANKED BUSINESS SCHOOL   **Right Place, MA**
Master of Business Administration, Marketing   May 2000
• Summa Cum Laude

EXCELLENT UNDERGRAD UNIVERSITY   **Partytown, PA**
Bachelor of Arts in Economics and Political Science   June 1991
• Dean's Honor List

<u>INTERESTS</u>
Dad of three; Avid runner and skier; Board Member at local YMCA

This is the resume of an experienced marketer.

GET THE DETAILS RIGHT

A resume should be easy to glance at and pick up top-line information: the companies you've worked at, the titles and responsibilities you've had, the length of employment, your education and leadership positions.

In terms of the style of your resume, it should above all be easy to read. It should use direct language, not corporate jargon that others might not know. Abbreviations that are second nature in your current company are Greek to everyone else.

At the bottom of many resumes is often a section called "Interests." It's just one line at the bottom. It might say that you're an avid marathoner or a cooking aficionado. These are important because, when you interview, they provide points of interest for the interviewer. Sometimes, it can also create a personal connection, as you may share passions.

This brings us to some of the golden rules:

- Don't BS on your resume. It's not ethical and there's always a chance you'll get called on it.
- Don't put "references available upon request." If they want them, they'll get them.
- Don't put your business contact information on your resume.
- Put months and years on your resume, otherwise the reader may assume you are trying to hide gaps. (For internships, it's okay to say "summer 2000" vs. months.)

Before you complete your resume and send it anywhere, ask mentors to review it and give advice on how you can make it stronger. Have someone who is highly detail-oriented read it for typos and inconsistencies. Make sure it represents you, that you're proud of it, and that you can speak to every bullet point it includes. Remember, an interviewer will highly likely say, "On your resume, I read that you did X, Y, Z. Tell me about that." Again, no BS.

APPLYING ONLINE

For an online application, you need an upfront section that bullet-points your skills and aligns them with what the job is calling for. This is critical because it's how artificial intelligence (AI) works. It looks for key relevant skills for every job.

The first task for an online resume is to get you past AI so you will have a human-eye look at your resume. Depending on what job you're applying for, you may have to add some bullets for the specific role. This is vital to get past the first screening.

AI is so important. For example, if one of my clients, a big-name company, posts a job online or on LinkedIn, they will likely get thousands of resumes. They don't have the capacity or the desire to look at all of them. The vast majority of the people who apply for roles are not good fits as they have neither the right backgrounds nor the right skillset. AI can be a very efficient way for companies to filter those candidates out. It screens the applications down to a manageable number. Customizing your resume as I suggest gives you a higher probability of making it past AI.

DEALING WITH GAPS

I'm often asked what to do about gaps in your resume. My advice is to work with your college career center or, later in your career, a quality recruiter. A good recruiter answers questions about your resume and has a write-up that speaks to the rationale for any gaps, such as having an ill family member, following a spouse's job, being a stay-at-home mom, taking a sabbatical, or traveling for a year.

If you don't work with a recruiter, you simply can put a line on your resume with an explanation, such as "Caretaker for ill family member," or "World Traveler 2015-17"—and leave it at that. That will have them nodding up and down, saying, "Okay, I understand that. Life happens." Those sorts of gaps won't exclude you from consideration if your background is strong.

If the gap was because you'd been fired from multiple jobs, and you just couldn't find one, that's going to be a tougher sell. Again, I suggest you talk with an executive recruiter and get their perspective. It might also be worth going back to reassess your strengths. You might be on the wrong career path altogether.

Having a strong resume is critical as your resume is your selling tool, and the reader is the buyer. Good salesmanship requires understanding what the reader wants to buy—and making sure you present that information clearly in your document.

Remember: Cover depth of your training, the breadth of your learning, and your relevant results.

While this chapter gives insight on how to write a strong resume, if you need extra help getting yours to the next level, our team can help you optimize it and get it into great shape. Simply follow this link: www.igniteyourcareerbook. com/resumes. Sign up, and we can help you create a killer resume.

A great resume will get you a "day in court" but it won't win you the case—or the job. In the next chapter, we'll look at how you can use networking to improve your chance of winning.

DOS AND DON'TS

My rules of thumb for resumes are simple and straightforward:

DOS	DON'TS
Do make your resume clean, clear, logical, and readable.	Don't try to make your resume cute, or fancy, or smell good.
Do use bullet points rather than paragraphs.	Don't put your picture on your resume.
Do cover breadth and depth of experience and accomplishments, with most recent experience first (except when right out of undergrad or graduate school).	Don't use long paragraphs. Don't use jargon or abbreviations nobody but your company understands.
Do use leadership prose, such as "lead," "develop," create," "initiate," "manage."	Don't send it off before you have others proofread it. Don't make it too long or too short.
Do make sure you're using the right tense, consistently, and have zero typos.	
Do add results wherever possible. Just as in real estate, where the key to success is "location, location, location," after the learning phase of your career, the key to success on your resume is "results, results, results."	

CHAPTER 6

BUILD YOUR NETWORKING MUSCLE

Networking is a critical tool for your job search, but it's more than that. You should see networking not simply as a tactic to use when you change jobs but as a foundation for broader success in your working life.

The benefits of networking:

- It's the process of developing your relationships to increase your business, enhance your knowledge, and expand your sphere of influence.
- It's a key strategy to build your connections and support in your industry.
- It's the cultivation of productive relationships for potential employment.

In some ways, networking is like exercise. You know it's good for you and that you should probably be doing more of it, but you can't get started or you don't feel like it. Just as exercise becomes a habit, you need to make networking a habit, too. Commit to networking and prioritize it as a way to help build your career.

WHEN AND HOW TO NETWORK

When? Now!

I network for a living, but you should start in college, or in your first job—in fact, wherever you are now! What matters is that you make networking a habit.

Some people are reluctant to reach out. It makes them feel uncomfortable. They may fear rejection, or feel they don't have any connections. But you already have more of a network than you think. You just haven't activated it yet.

Most people are very open to networking, and there are a number of ways to find them. You can reach out to family and friends in your chosen industry or contact alumni from your high school, college, or grad school. Many schools have alumni offices that can provide email addresses and telephone numbers, and you can also connect with alumni via tools like LinkedIn or Facebook. Some colleges also have mentoring programs where alumni opt in and raise their hand to help students from their school. They truly want to help.

How? Send them a note via email or LinkedIn.

Introduce yourself as a student from their school interested in entering their industry. Ask if they might be willing to speak with you in order to share their journey, give advice on how to navigate your career, and suggest any other individuals you might speak to. Don't ask them to hire you, although you could ask what their company looks for in employees. After your conversation, if they think you might be a good fit, they will offer it up.

Ask if you might keep them apprised of your career journey and reach back out to them for advice. Write them notes, thanking them for their time, advice, and guidance. Ask them for suggestions on great industry books to read. Stay in touch. The easiest way to do this is to put a reminder on your calendar for two to three months out to update them; include notes about your conversation in the reminder to make it really easy to go back to what they shared with you, what you've learned, and where you are in your journey. Keep good track of who you spoke with, their background, their telephone number, their email, and what they had to offer.

That's how you start building your networking muscle and

creating a habit that will expand your connections. You should plan to keep the process going throughout your career, not simply when you're looking for a job.

It goes without saying that you would not attempt a triathlon without extensive preparation. To do otherwise would result in failing miserably or even getting hurt. You need to train constantly to reach your goal.

The same goes for networking. You reap the greatest rewards by taking the steps to prepare for your "race"—which is the time you actually need a job. If you've done all the work to prepare your network, winning when it counts will be so much easier. If you wait until you need a job to do your preparation, you may not have enough networking muscle to get the job you want.

A FARMING ANALOGY

One of the analogies we use in recruiting is related to farming. A farmer has to prepare the ground, plant the seed, then cultivate, weed, water, and nurture the crops in order to reap a bountiful harvest. He can't idle through the spring and summer, then simply throw seed on the ground at the start of fall and expect to reap a harvest two weeks later. He has to work hard and plan ahead to get the greatest rewards.

A CASE STUDY

If you've done your preparation, then once you're ready to

search for a job, you can simply dial up your networking activities. You can reach out in a more targeted way because you've cultivated your relationships.

My daughter's story is a great case study. As she was heading to graduation from a liberal arts school, she decided that she wanted to find a job in the music industry in Nashville. Her school had a strong career center, but it had no focus on the music industry, and most of the companies that recruited on campus were from the Northeast, where the school was located, rather than the Southeast.

This is how my daughter started networking. In January, before she graduated, she reached out to her high school and college alumni offices and got the name and email address of every single alumni who currently lived in Nashville, whatever industry they were in. She then sent out hundreds of emails asking people if they might be willing to talk to her or meet to share their story and give her advice.

She had fifteen to twenty informational calls with people from all industries who had great advice and shared their contacts in the music industry. She went to Nashville for a long weekend in March, by which time she had connected with key contacts to schedule multiple informational interviews in the music industry. Finally, she moved to Nashville in July. She had no job at the time, but she had continued her intense networking and arranged multiple interviews.

Within two weeks, she had two job offers. She accepted a job at a great company that was eventually bought out by a huge music label.

My daughter's networking paid off. It had taken real commitment, however. The whole process had begun seven months before she needed a job.

After her own journey, she now says, "I'm happy to network with anybody. If they call me and ask, 'Can you share your journey with me and how you got where you are, what you've learned in the music industry, what advice would you give me?' I'm all in and I'm going to do everything I can to help them achieve their goals. But if they call me and say, 'Can you get me a job?' it irritates me, and I don't want to help them."

That brings us to one of the golden rules. Don't treat networking like it's all about you. It needs to be an exchange.

Other common mistakes to avoid:

- Not asking for help.
- Failing to keep in touch, or only reaching out when you need something.
- Not writing thank-you notes when people offer time, advice, or assistance.
- Not helping others. "All about me" really turns people off.

- Only networking when you need a job, because people can sense desperation.
- Not networking on an ongoing basis. You need to keep using that muscle and make it part of your weekly plan.

I CAN'T NETWORK (OR I WON'T)

It may be that you feel very uncomfortable networking. You may not have the confidence to pick up the phone to call a stranger. You don't need to worry. It doesn't come naturally to most people. People who are innately outgoing and have a strong sales persona might be comfortable with it, but the rest of us are not. The easiest way to do it is to reach out to networks where you have something in common with people (family friends, school alumni, or friends of friends), because those folks are inclined to want to help in the first place, so it's less intimidating to contact them.

I know from experience that if you've watched a friend's child grow up, you are happy to help. I have helped friends often as they call me and say, "My son is lost and doesn't know what to do. Can he come and sit down with you?" I love it. Not only can I help young people think through things; I can also make them accountable to me. If their parents push them, it's irritating. I can say, "Okay, I've invested my time with you. This is what I'm asking in return. I want a weekly report of everybody you've reached out to, interviews you've had, and what's happened. When you have an interview, I want you to let me know so I can help prep you." It's rewarding to see them knuckle down and eventually find a great opportunity.

My kids have gotten great internships thanks to alumni from their school or friends of the family, and I have helped people get internships in turn. It always feels amazing to pay it forward.

Another example is about one of my sons. Years ago, I was talking to a candidate who was telling me how much he loved working at Amazon. I happened to ask him, "Does Amazon hire undergrads?" He said, "We do, and I think we have the strongest undergrad training program in the country. It's incredibly robust and people get a lot of responsibility." I said to him, "My son is in his senior year. If he were interested, would you be open to speaking to him?" He replied, "I'd be happy to."

They spoke and he must have been impressed because he asked for my son's resume. After that, my son went through the entire interview process and ended up getting a job and loving his experience at Amazon.

While it is great to leverage contacts, it's important to know that they can only open the door and make introductions; they can't get anyone a job. If you're not capable or haven't done your homework, you're not getting the job.

NETWORKING FOR LIFE

There are different ways to keep networking throughout your career. The key is that once you're in your chosen job and industry, you don't stop networking. Keep it going. Almost all people who are successful in their careers have built an incredible network in their industry outside their current company or job.

One way to do this is to invite people in your network for coffee. Get to know them and their story. Ask for and share advice on the industry, companies, career pathing, vendors, anything. Soak in their knowledge and stay in touch with them.

A second way is to keep mining your alumni network: high school, college, grad school. You have something in common with all of them. Again, you can go back to family contacts. Don't forget the professionals who have known you since you were a baby. They may well be excited to be part of your journey and help you succeed.

A third way is through industry events, such as talks, mixers, or conferences. Even if you're a little shy and introverted, stretch yourself. This is a great way to meet people in an atmosphere in which everyone has put their hand up to talk to new people.

There are some tricks of the trade for industry and alumni events:

- Do homework beforehand on who will be attending, and have relevant questions for them.
- Ask open-ended questions, instead of talking about yourself. What is their role? What trends have they noticed? What advice would they share? What have they learned from mistakes they've made along the way? People like to talk, and even if you say very little, they will think of you fondly because you cared enough to ask about them and their ideas.
- Remember that you don't have to talk a lot. By asking insightful questions, you'll build the relationship. When they want to know about you, it will be one-on-one with someone you're already familiar with, so it will be easy.
- Always follow up with the people you talk to. Thank them for their time and keep them updated on your career journey.

A fourth way to keep networking is to be strategically active on LinkedIn. Once you have started on your career, post or share relevant articles once or twice a week, so you keep coming up on the feed, and like and comment on other people's posts. Try to build your network in your industry by inviting people to link in with you. Write a note when you invite them, because it increases the likelihood that they'll accept. Say something like, "Hi. I love your profile. I'm impressed by it. I'm xxxx in your industry and would love to link in with you and learn from your posts and experience."

As you build your network and see articles or postings that impress you, you can both comment on them and message the person directly. You could say something like, "Your article really resonated with me. I appreciate your insights, and I'm wondering if you might be willing to have a fifteen-minute conversation just to share your wisdom with somebody junior in the industry." Finally, you should join industry groups where you can meet peers and further build your network.

In conclusion, networking can be a huge asset throughout your career. When you think about networking, remember to focus on building your networking muscle and continuously farming, preparing your ground, and planning ahead, so that you reap great rewards from your efforts. At the very least, you will gain more knowledge, which can be priceless in itself. That will pay off when it is time to apply for jobs, which is what we'll cover in the next chapter.

DOS AND DON'TS

Here are some dos and don'ts of networking:

DOS	DON'TS
Do start networking early and make it a habit—build that muscle!	Don't be too lazy or afraid to network.
Do tap into family friends, alumni from your schools, and people you've worked with in the past.	Don't make networking all about you. Don't wait until you need a job to start networking.
Do focus on learning from others rather than expecting them to get you a job.	Don't forget to thank people and keep them apprised of your progress.
Do thank people, stay in touch, and pay it forward.	Don't forget to pay it forward.

CHAPTER 7

———

BOOSTING THE ODDS

There are different ways to apply for jobs, but the key is to avoid going into the dreaded black hole. Once your application is in there, it's never coming out. That's why applying for a job is a little bit like gambling or playing the lottery. The difference is that in your job search you can improve the odds.

In this chapter, I'll show you how to play the game intelligently to increase your chances of winning.

There are three common ways to apply for a job:

1. Online
2. Through friends or contacts
3. Via an executive recruiter

ONLINE

The most common way to apply for a job today is online. You'll find opportunities on LinkedIn; job boards, such as Career Builder or Indeed; or a company website. These venues provide the easiest type of application to complete, but they also have the lowest probability of success.

Sometimes it just feels good to push that button and send something off. It feels like you're taking a positive step. I appreciate that, but my best advice is that these job listings rarely net a winning hand, and should only be used as a last resort.

Many companies use artificial intelligence (AI) or applicant tracking systems (ATS) to scan the thousands of resumes they receive. It's a way to reduce the number of resumes an actual human will have to review to a manageable amount.

If you decide you are going to apply online, the key is to get a real person to assess your resume. It's not easy, but there are ways you can increase the chances of getting past AI or ATS:

- Check the company's website before you apply. This gives you a chance to learn their mission and values so that you can talk to them in a cover letter. It also demonstrates interest, as they can check who has been looking at their website.

- If a cover letter is requested, write one that is clear and specific to your accomplishments and skills, but that also addresses the needs of the specific job and your interest in their specific organization. Make sure it is well-written and has no typos.
- Update your resume by tailoring it with keywords from the job description you are applying for, because the words in the job description are what the AI programs look for.
- If you're applying via the company's website and you need to fill out an application form, fill it out fully with no typos.
- Clean up your social media presence. If you make it past AI to a real person, trust me, they will always check you out. Even though you may think your Facebook page or Instagram is private, they can get to it. Get rid of any inappropriate pictures or tweets that are not professional in nature. You want to come across as being professional and somebody who fits the company culture.
- Keep an ongoing log of where you've sent your resume, when and how you sent it, and what job you applied for.
- Do not try to get your resume into a company through three, four, or five different avenues. This will not be seen as a positive and may stop your progress forward.
- Also know that online job postings are often out-of-date, forgotten attempts by companies to build their database, or a required external job posting before they hire an internal candidate.

FRIENDS AND CONTACTS

The second way of applying for a job has a higher probability of success. This is applying via former work colleagues, friends, college career centers or professors, or individuals with whom you've networked. These contacts do not just increase the probability that your resume will be reviewed by an actual human rather than AI; they can help get your resume to the right people.

If you've worked with a person previously, this is the best scenario and has the highest odds of success as they can speak to your experiences, abilities, and fit with the company. Friends may be able to speak only to your perceived fit with the company culture, but that is in turn preferable to somebody you've just networked with.

One note. When you ask somebody to advocate on your behalf, you're asking them to vouch for you. Their credibility is on the line as well as yours, so be mindful of that and respect their position. At the same time, be mindful that they may have limited influence to pass on your resume. It might never reach the decision maker, which is why applying through a recruiter is the best bet when possible.

EXECUTIVE RECRUITER

The third way to apply for a job is through a quality executive recruiter. Many people have negative perceptions of executive recruiters or headhunters, and I admit that there are bad ones out there. But there are a lot of quality recruiters, too, and finding one in your industry who you trust, who wants to know not just about your background but also about your goals and aspirations, can be life-altering.

To find professional recruiters, I recommend these steps:

- Look online for executive recruiters in your field. If their website is professional and well done, they likely are reputable.
- Ask your professor if he or she knows anyone you might speak to, as they might have come from the industry or can contact previous students on your behalf.
- Contact alumni in your area of expertise and ask them for a referral. (I have many interns contact me from recommendations they get from their bosses over the summer.)

Great recruiters are partners in your career. They will not only help you find jobs, but can also counsel you on potential moves, help you negotiate offers, and eventually, as you move into your leveraging phase, help you build your own team. One of my candidates, whom I have placed numerous times and also helped build his own teams, is currently a chief marketing officer at a private equity company. He says, "I would not be where I am in my career without Kris and the O'Connell Group. She has placed me numerous times, offered meaningful counsel throughout my career, and built my organization at three companies."

When recruiters have been hired by a company to bring forward a slate of qualified and interested candidates, they're a great resource for candidates. Not only do they have a direct line to the hiring manager and decision makers; they are also the strategic partner in the hire, so they can advocate on your behalf. If you have any gaps on your resume or things that need explaining, recruiters can often take the issue off the table before you get knocked out.

Quality executive recruiters can also help with other elements that will further increase your probability of success, such as resume writing, interview preparation, negotiation assistance, and even helping you positively manage your resignation. It's like having a personal coach who can help you enhance all your career capabilities.

The best of all worlds and the approach with the highest probability of success is having an executive recruiter working with you, *and* also knowing someone in the company who can advocate on your behalf. This is what we call the push–pull: the recruiter speaks to your skills, ability, and fit, while your friend talks to the fit as well. This is when you hold the winning hand and have the best chance to interview for the job.

YOU'RE IN CHARGE

It is worth underlining here that this is *your* job search. Your resume is yours to decide when, where, and how you want to apply. There are some unethical recruiters who will send your resume in without your permission. Make sure that you only send your resume to recruiters you trust. Be explicit that you're giving them permission to send you in to the company you agreed on and no other. And keep very good track so you are the one in control.

Be strategic in your job search and increase the probability for success by getting to know quality executive recruiters in your field and utilizing past work associates, friends, and networking relationships.

Only as a last resort should you apply directly for a job through an online listing.

However you apply, you will never get a job without a successful interview. In the next chapter, I'll explain the different types of interviews and how to prepare and increase your chances of success.

DOS AND DON'TS

Here are some dos and don'ts of applying for jobs:

DOS	DON'TS
Do keep track of every place you've applied: when, who, how, and where.	Don't just apply online because it feels good to do something.
Do call your recruiter before you apply online to see if they're working on the job, or if they know senior leaders in the company and would send you in with permission.	Don't forget to keep people who have advocated for you up to date on your progress. Don't forget to update and clean up your social profiles.
Do always see if you know somebody in the company who can advocate for you or deliver your resume to the hiring manager before you apply for a job online.	Don't mark your LinkedIn page as "seeking a job," unless you are either not working or you're okay with your current company knowing you want to leave.
Do tailor your resume to the job you're applying for, which is especially critical if you are applying online.	

CHAPTER 8

THE INTERVIEW

So, you have a strong resume, you've networked and identified a great opportunity, and now you've been invited to interview. Congratulations!

But you can't let up here! There is still critical work to be done.

A successful interview is key to receiving an offer. That's why this is the longest chapter in the book. Don't worry, though. With a little coaching, it's not too difficult—but it is worth mastering because this is the make or break moment. I've seen perfect candidates miss out on jobs because they did not get on top of the interview process.

The key is preparation.

The first part of this chapter is about doing homework on yourself and the company. In the second section, I'll take you through typical questions you might be asked and how to ask appropriate questions yourself that will continue to sell you. We'll wrap up by looking at different types of interviews and how best to prepare for them.

PREP FOR THE INTERVIEW

Interview preparation is absolutely critical in your job search. Expecting to be successful in an interview without doing any prep is like wanting to be a premier college or pro athlete without extensive training and a huge commitment of time and energy. Preparation is how you can differentiate yourself from others and put yourself at the front of the pack. This is your chance to bring your talents and experience to life—but only if you do the work and put in the effort.

DON'T JUST WOO THEM. WOW THEM!

I believe that interviewing is a combination of wooing and wowing.

As you'll recall from chapter 1, WOO is a quality in the StrengthsFinder assessment that stands for *winning others over*, similar to the word "woo" itself. Wooing is when you leave an interview with them saying, "Joe's great. I'd love to have him on my team, love to go for a beer with him, love to hang out." In other words, they think you fit. Wooing is connecting with a person, fitting the company culture, and having them like you. People are much happier when they work with people they like, so if somebody has two candidates that are equally capable, they will lean into the person they liked better.

Wowing is leaving the same interview with them saying, "Joe's great, and I believe he could deliver great results in our business." It is being able to articulate your experiences, your strengths, and your achievements in a way that leads an interviewer to believe you could do a great job in a role and that you have growth potential for the future.

We'll focus more here on wowing, but wooing is also critical. I am surprised by how many times in my twenty-five-plus years in recruiting that people have lost a job they should have gotten because they didn't master wooing. These are some of the ways they blew it:

- One candidate was rude to a waitress during a lunch interview.
- Another got mad on the phone with the hotel, airline, and travel agent when their travel plans went wrong, and these people represent the company.
- Another got impatient with the receptionist at the company because the interviews were running late.
- One woman had a great interview, then called her fiancé

from the back of the limo on the way to the airport, and boasted how she had the interviewers eating out of the palm of her hand. "I am the bomb," she told him. The driver overheard her and mentioned it to the company president, whom he drove to the airport weekly. The company had an offer prepared for her, but they did not extend it.

I share this to stress that every touchpoint counts. Every single interaction you have with a potential employer or their representatives builds or takes away from your equity, so you need to keep them positive.

Wooing is showing up well prepared, dressed appropriately, and being enthusiastic about the company and the job. They want to know you care. If you don't, they won't. Being well prepared will also enable you to feel more confident and comfortable. Finally, connecting with others during each interview and interaction is critical.

Be mindful of all of this, and you'll have wooing down pat.

Now for WOWING.

Suppose someone asks about your strengths and accomplishments, and you list them. If they are asked ten minutes later what you said, they won't remember. They'd be like a *deer caught in the headlights*. On the other hand, if you were to say, "Here are my top three strengths and let me tell you a quick story of how each of them has allowed me to deliver success," they'll remember your stories. When you paint a vivid picture through stories, something happens in the brain that allows your listener to remember—and believe.

USING STAR TO BE A STAR

You want your stories to resonate with the interviewer. You can do this by telling your stories using the STAR Plus storytelling method. STAR is an acronym that stands for the four components of this method:

1. Situation: What is the background information of the story?
2. Thinking: This is the analysis or research you did, the trend you noted, or an observation that someone in your company shared with you. It is the "aha" or "eureka" moment when the proverbial light bulb goes off.
3. Action: These are the steps you then took.
4. Result: This is the success you delivered.

The STAR Plus method includes one more component:

5. Learning: If you learned something along the way that led you to do things differently in the future, you can share that as well. We all learn by making mistakes, and learning and adapting is how we improve and get better.

You can use the STAR method strategically for interviews. I have candidates focus their STAR Plus stories on both their strengths and accomplishments.

Here's how:

WRITING YOUR STAR STORIES: STRENGTHS

- Pull out four or five index cards (they force you to be succinct), grab your resume, and think of the things you are innately good at and how they set you up for success.
- Write one strength at the top of each card.
- Underneath, write a story in the STAR format that demonstrates how that strength allowed you to succeed.
- If you have an example of learning that will help you improve in the future, quickly mention it.

- Each story should be 1–1½ minutes long. Too short and your interviewer won't believe you; too long and their eyes will glaze over. If they have questions, they'll ask for more details.
- You MUST practice out loud until you can tell the story without rambling or stumbling.

WRITING YOUR STAR STORIES: ACCOMPLISHMENTS

Next, you'll want to do the same thing with your accomplishments. Think of your success stories. They don't have to be earth-shattering. It may be where you won over other interns who originally were competitive and brought them together to jointly achieve a goal.

- Write each story on an index card in the STAR format. (The only difference from the strength cards is that these can be 1½–2 minutes long, as the explanations tend to be a bit more involved.)
- At the bottom of each card, write one or two strengths that helped you achieve the goal. The reason I suggest you put the strengths on the bottom of these cards is that people hire you for your skills and abilities. The more you can link skills and experiences to achievements, the more powerful they become.
- Again, practice telling your stories out loud until they click.

The beauty of creating these index cards is that they are very versatile. They can be used to help you answer behavioral questions easily, as well as questions about strengths and accomplishments. You can use them to prepare for questions such as:

- Tell me about a time you had to win someone over.
- Tell me about a time when you had to sell management on an idea.
- Tell me about a time when you failed but course-corrected and ultimately succeeded.

The more cards you write, the more stories you can tell, the better you will know yourself and perform in the interview. Also, make sure to keep your cards forever, so you don't have to recreate them later.

Your stories paint a picture of you. They bring your strengths, skills, capabilities, and achievements to life. In the marketing world, you are the "brand," and the stories on your index cards are "the reason to believe."

INTERVIEWING IS LIKE DATING

I strongly believe that interviewing is very much like dating. Your goal is to get the company to fall in love with you and ask you to marry them (or at least, go to work there). You then can decide if you want to accept their "proposal."

There is a truism that is relevant here: "People like people who like them." In interview terms, this means, do your homework on the organization.

Over the years, too many companies have come back to me after an interview and said that a candidate was great, smart, and a good fit. However, the company wasn't moving forward with an offer because the candidate "doesn't know anything about our company or our brands." The company concluded that the candidate was not truly interested in joining their organization.

At the very least, go to the organization's website and read their value statement. If you know anyone who works there, talk to them. In your interview, demonstrate a sincere interest in the company. Making you an offer is not just a business decision for them. It's far more emotional than that. They're invested in whether or not you take the job, and whether you're excited about *their* organization.

In my world, which is marketing in consumer goods, I tell candidates: "Go to the grocery store, Sam's Club, and look at Amazon. Look at their products and their competitors. Come up with ideas about what they do well and some opportunity areas."

This is an approach that works across industries. Map out strengths and weaknesses of the company you're interviewing with, and assess their competitors. That's how you show you've really done your homework.

It goes without saying that you should not say negative things about the company's products. Be positive rather than critical. Highlight a trend and suggest one or two possible areas to explore.

Another thing I recommend before your first "date" is to do a mock interview with someone your trust, or video yourself answering questions. When I was at Kellogg Business School, I had a mock interview. When I watched myself on video, I was shocked to see that I would unconsciously link my hands in front of me, as if I was praying. As I answered questions I was excited about, my fingers would stay linked and my hands would rise in front of my face. I had no idea I was doing that. Once I saw it, I made sure my hands were down by my sides. I still used them as visuals, but they were no longer so distracting or in front of my face. Mock interviews help you get the kinks out.

COMMON INTERVIEW QUESTIONS

There are a number of questions that often come up in various forms during interviews. It's worth thinking about them ahead of time and having answers ready.

TELL ME ABOUT YOURSELF AND WALK ME THROUGH YOUR RESUME

These are two questions that are very similar, and that truly merge at college. The key here is to make the answers succinct—thirty seconds—as they can easily go out of control.

Tell me about yourself. This gives you a chance to show where you come from and the values that shape you. You are trying to show yourself as unique and memorable.

For example, I once did a session with doctors preparing to interview for their next rotation. We discussed their stories. One person had decided she wanted to be a doctor because she grew up on a farm; birthing animals got her into medicine. Another person was from India and had witnessed terrible illness there. He wanted eventually to bring back his expertise to India.

Stories like these make you more memorable. They differentiate you.

My thirty-second story is this:

> "I grew up in Saint Louis, Missouri. Both my parents owned their own business. So, early on, I had exposure to business and entrepreneurialism. I was very active in sports in high school and was captain of most of my teams. I also ran a camp for inner city kids during the summer, which is what led me

to believe I wanted to go into child psychology, which is one of the reasons I went to Tufts University. At Tufts, I majored in psychology and loved it, but somewhere along the way, I realized I didn't want to be a therapist and listen to peoples' problems all day. That's when I shifted my focus to business, likely from the influence of my parents and my competitive spirit and leadership capabilities."

If it fits naturally, do not be afraid to use humor. It makes people like you more and relate to you.

Walk me through your resume. The response to this is a quick overview of your college, internship, or work experiences and passions, as well as any leadership or impactful roles you held. With internships and work experience, talk about roles you had, skills you developed, major achievements, and why you left the role (you don't need to explain why you left summer internships).

You should make your answers both short and sweet: no more than three minutes combined. (Interviewers complain to me when I send them a candidate who gave a twenty-minute monologue. This is brutal for the candidate and the interviewer.)

Think about the questions beforehand, write out your answers, make them short, and practice them. This is your show, so you need to have done your rehearsal. The interviewer will probe along the way if they need more detail.

TELL ME ABOUT A MISTAKE YOU HAVE MADE

Everyone makes mistakes. It's how we learn. The key is not to make the same mistake twice. Interviewers want to hear quickly about a real mistake. The key to answering this question well is to explain what you learned from your mistake and how you course-corrected.

WHAT ARE YOUR WEAKNESSES?

There are several ways of handling this question:

A weakness that you have rectified: Even though the weakness was in the past, it shows how you can take the bull by the horns, and how you don't look to others to solve your problems.

For example, when I was at business school, I was fine at doing presentations, but when I went to work at Kraft, I saw that the superstars were phenomenal presenters. I wanted to be a superstar, too, so I signed up for Toastmasters and Presentation Skills. I sat down with my boss and told him about my goal, and he sent me out to ten markets to introduce a new product. Within six months, I'd converted that opportunity area into a strength.

A developmental weakness: This weakness stems from lack of experience. Here you can give an example of a skill you recently learned and describe how you proactively built the "muscle" of that skill. Explain how you continue to apply the same determination to building other skills as you gain more experience, turning your weaknesses into strengths. This is called "bridging." You use past performance as an indicator of future performance.

An example of this would be a junior marketer who shared that they had not yet worked on TV advertising. They could say something like, "I haven't had the opportunity to work on TV advertising yet, but I was recently exposed to customer marketing. Here are the steps I took to convert that from a developmental area to a strength. I spent a week going out with the sales force and I went with the customer marketing team on multiple buyers' calls. I also worked with the shopper team for a week. Doing these things got me up to speed really quickly and helped me understand how to be successful in the customer marketing role. I believe that once I'm exposed to advertising, I will take similar steps to close that gap."

A weakness that you manage so it does not get in the way of your success: An example of this is taken from President Obama (love him or hate him, he did a nice job on this answer). When he was asked this question in 2008, he had a good answer. He said, "My weakness is details.

I'm a big-picture guy. I don't like details and I'm not good at them." He went on to say that he hired people who were detailed oriented, who were great project managers who loved to handle all the minutiae. Together, he said, they made a great team.

Another example is from one of my candidates who told me, "My weakness, which is an area I'm always working on and managing, is that I'm a little shy and introverted. It depends on the situation, but what I've learned to do is to build relationships with people one on one, because I excel at that. Then when I'm in big groups, it's not as overwhelming, because I have foundational relationships with everybody. Because these people are all my friends and have my back, and I have relationships with them, I am then able to manage that part of my personality, so it doesn't get in the way of my success."

Be sure to use examples that are appropriate for where you are in your career. At the learning phase (chapter 2), we have many weaknesses due to lack of work experience and exposure. So be smart here: Don't pick a showstopper that will make people think twice about hiring you. Instead, think clearly about your weaknesses and isolate the ones you've already overcome during college, grad school, an internship, or previous job.

WHAT COMPANY DO YOU THINK DOES A GOOD JOB IN YOUR INDUSTRY?

Your natural inclination might be to use the company you're interviewing with, but it often makes sense here to speak about another industry and company. The key here is to clearly describe the qualities that seem to make that company strong and successful.

WHAT LEADERS DO YOU ADMIRE AND WHY?

Be thoughtful about your answer, but whomever you choose, it is important to give specific reasons for your choice. Also, it is a good idea to be able to describe the leader in terms of a company culture similar to that of the company you're interviewing with.

WHAT TYPE OF CULTURE DO YOU WORK BEST IN?

Here, you should have done your homework and know the company culture. You need to make sure that your answer ties into both your and their cultural values, because you want to be the one deciding, "Do I want to work here?"

WHAT ARE YOUR COMPENSATION EXPECTATIONS?

US laws are changing, and in many states, companies are no longer allowed to ask you your current compensation or compensation history. Instead, they may proactively ask your salary expectations. If they do, say something like this:

- Compensation is important to me, but it is a piece of a larger puzzle.
- I'm also looking for the right company, the right culture, and the right opportunity, both today and in the long term.
- I'm confident that if we want to make it work, we can find a win-win solution.

They may still probe for what would be acceptable to you, so do your research so you know the range for the job. Be realistic, because if your figure is too high, you'll take yourself out of the running.

Realistically, when you're coming out of college or graduate school, the compensation is set. They may share it and ask, "Are you okay with this?" Negotiation about compensation is more usual when you're shifting to your second job and beyond. When you are graduating college or grad school, you might be able to negotiate a start date or planned vacation, but not much else.

A couple of final tips in case you feel that you are not answering questions well:

- If you find yourself rambling and not answering the

question asked, stop yourself and say: "My sense is I am not addressing your question; could you possibly rephrase it, as I truly want to address what you are looking for." This shows self-awareness and confidence and gives you a chance to actually answer their question.

- If you are nervous and worried about how you are coming across, say something like: "I apologize if I am nervous. I am just so excited about this opportunity and feel it is an amazing fit." They will likely say something like, "Don't worry. I just want to get to know you and your experiences." And your nerves will go away!

YOUR OWN QUESTIONS

After interviewing you, the interviewer will ask, "Do you have any questions for me?"

I believe that the best response is: "Yes, but before I ask my questions, I want to make sure I have answered all of your questions, as I am really excited about your company and this role. If there are any areas we have not covered or answers I gave that you were not comfortable with, I would rather revisit those." This allows you to demonstrate your interest. They will either say, "Well, we did not cover X," or "No, I am good."

When you do ask questions, remember that this is another chance to continue selling yourself. People who don't keep this in mind both miss opportunities to sell and can even lose job opportunities.

Most importantly, there are some questions to avoid at this point in the process. I call them WIIFM questions: "What's in it for me?" Here are a few WIIFM questions you should not ask:

- What are the typical hours at your company?
- What is your 401(k) match?
- How much vacation do I get?
- What are typical raises here?
- What is the average bonus payment?

Never ask a WIIFM question during an interview. If you receive an offer, then WIIFM questions are fair game and you should ask them. I advise candidates to start a WIIFM folder. As you think of questions, add them to the folder; when you get an offer, out they come.

When you prepare questions to ask in your interview, remember that your goal is to show the interviewer you are smart, strategic, and that you've done your homework.

Ask questions linking trends to their business. Here are a few examples taken from the consumer marketing industry:

- Given that the organic/natural trend seems to be

becoming mainstream, are you planning on entering
this category either through innovation or acquisition?
- I have noticed in other categories that X is hot—would
this ingredient fit within your brand essence?
- Fiber and protein are growing in popularity—have you
seen this trend in your segment?

Ask something about their values and how they come to
life at the company.

Make sure to ask one question about the company's culture,
such as: "Culture is an important element to me. Can you
describe what sort of person excels at your company, or
why you love it here?"

TYPES OF INTERVIEWS

There are a range of interview types that might take place
during your job search:

- Telephone screen
- Video screen/Zoom
- One-on-one in-person interview
- In-person panel interview
- Case study: individual or group

TELEPHONE SCREEN

Here it is important to be in a place where you have good versus spotty reception. You also want to take the call somewhere quiet, without distraction or external noises.

Key Tips

- Smile as you answer questions; it actually comes across on the phone.
- Be high energy and excited on the phone.
- Actively listen to the questions and ask for clarification if you are not sure what they are looking for.
- Wait a second before you answer a question to make sure you do not speak over the interviewer.
- Have your index cards in front of you to use during a phone interview.
- Don't forget to ask the interviewer for their email at the end of the call so you can write them a thank-you note.

VIDEO SCREEN

Video screens (VS) are becoming very common. We have some clients who are even extending offers after multiple VS interviews, and I expect this trend will continue.

Some interviewers use automated VS/AI to cull down candidates to a manageable number. Here you often have eight questions you answer on video (you're not given them ahead of time). You are given two or three minutes to answer each question, and you likely have one do-over per question. If you don't like how you answered it the first time, push "start over." Do homework so you can have an idea of the questions that might be asked and can prepare for them ahead of time.

A "real" person VS is closer to an in-person interview, so you want to prepare in a very similar manner (as described earlier in this chapter).

Again, whether with a person or AI, it's very important to have done your homework, to be articulate and engaging, and to be dressed professionally (more on this later).

Key Tips

- Look at the camera, not the screen. If you look at the monitor, it appears that you're looking away from the interviewer.
- Mind your background, as your surroundings say a lot about you. Position yourself in front of a blank wall or a warm one-color background, without distracting objects or pictures. Make sure there's plenty of light in the room.
- Add extra enthusiasm. All newscasters know that their reactions come off differently on screen, so compensate with extra enthusiasm and concise answers.

- Slow down. It can be easy to talk over people on a video call, so wait to respond until after the interviewer has stopped speaking.
- Beware of interruptions. Don't forget to turn off your phone and warn your family that you'll need privacy.
- Conduct a mock interview. Try a run-through on Skype or your video conferencing app with a trusted friend or colleague. Ask them for an honest assessment of how you did to iron out inevitable mistakes. It will also help you feel more relaxed knowing that the technology works.
- Dress for success. Wear just what you would wear for a real interview.
- Put your hands where they can see them. Remember that a high proportion of communication comes from body language and other nonverbal clues, so make sure they can see the whole top half of your body.
- Pay attention to the details. Use a simple account name—your first and last names are fine—and have a nice picture that shows only you.
- Check your tech. Make sure that you have a good computer connection and that your wireless connection won't slow you down. Also make sure that your computer has plenty of battery power. Arrive early, as you would for a face-to-face interview. Logging on ten minutes ahead of time also gives you time to troubleshoot any last-minute technical issues.

IN-PERSON INTERVIEW

Here you are meeting with one person at a time. Remember to smile, shake their hand firmly, if appropriate, and look them in the eye. Be professional but also be yourself during the interview. Remember that you want to both woo and wow them. At the end of the interview, thank them for their time and tell them again how interested you are in the role and company. Ask them for their business card and, if they do not have it, their email address. That way you can send them a thank-you email note within twenty-four hours.

PANEL INTERVIEW

This can be anything from two to six people interviewing you at the same time. It can feel very intimidating, but once you've done the first one you'll see its merits. It is actually a very efficient way for you to show your stuff to more people, and it can be a more relaxed interview.

Keep these factors in mind:

- They are not trying to intimidate you with a panel interview. They are simply being efficient with your time and theirs.
- Answer whoever asked the question and then pause for probing from others.
- The others will be listening but also thinking about the next question to ask.

CASE INTERVIEW

This can either be an individual or a group case interview:

- Individual Case Study: In-depth case studies are used in some industries, such as consulting and investment banking. If you are focusing in these areas, check with your career center. Otherwise, companies are looking to understand your thought process rather than looking for a right or wrong answer. They might ask off-the-wall questions to see how you wrestle with an intellectual challenge. Examples could be:
  - How many cats are there in the US?
  - How many windshield wipers are there in the US?
  - You have a lemonade stand for the second year. Sales are up but profits are down. What might be going on?
- Group Case Study: Here you will be in a room with other potential candidates and you will be given a case study to evaluate. They are likely watching you as you work. They will be looking at how you work with others and what role you assume. They will also be looking at how you tackle the case study as a team and build on each other's ideas.

YOUR APPEARANCE

Unless a company tells you otherwise, the expectation is that you come for an interview in professional attire. That means a suit for men, and either a suit or a professional dress for women.

Sometimes, companies tell you, "Do not wear a suit, because you'll stick out like a sore thumb." In that case, wear business casual. The other extreme is like when my son interviewed at Amazon and they told him, "Do not wear a suit. You can wear anything from shorts, T-shirts, and flip-flops, to khakis and a polo."

The safest approach is to assume business-professional, unless told otherwise. (Even for Amazon, I would err on the side of khakis and a polo shirt.)

In summary, there are many types of interviews. Whatever type, however, interview preparation is critical. Not prepping would be as foolish as getting into Harvard and leaving one class before you get your degree. Invest in yourself, practice, and bring to life what makes you unique and special. Many of the skills you gain from learning how to interview well will also help you in life, such as presenting yourself well, answering questions succinctly, and always treating others with respect.

If you have done your homework but still feel you need some coaching, sign up for our interview guidance at www. igniteyourcareerbook.com/interview-prep. The more preparation you do, the higher your chance of success—

and of moving on to the stage we will discuss in chapter 9, negotiating an offer.

DOS AND DON'TS

The significant dos and don'ts for interviewing are as follows:

DOS	DON'TS
Do focus on woo and wow.	Don't be flippant or cocky.
Do connect and be respectful of everyone you meet.	Don't be longwinded.
Do homework on yourself and the company.	Don't dress casually, even if it is their company attire, unless they tell you to.
Do be concise and focus on results where you have them.	Don't try to BS through an answer.
Do practice out loud to work out kinks in your stories.	Don't look at your phone during the interview.
Do be energetic and excited about the company and role.	
Do write email thank-you notes within twenty-four hours of the interview.	
Do be yourself; be a real authentic person.	

CHAPTER 9

WIN–WIN NEGOTIATION

If things go well and you receive an offer, the next stage of a job search is often negotiation, when you and the company agree on the terms of your employment. This normally takes place at the end of the process, but sometimes the human resources team or recruiter will calibrate you along the way. They do this to try to avoid a situation where their company or client falls in love with a candidate who will not accept their offer.

Applicants often think negotiations are just about salary. Of course, salary is a key element, but you can negotiate many other things, such as sign-on bonus, vacation, equity amount, and start date. As a recent graduate, you will not likely be negotiating salary with large corporations, as their entry salaries are usually predetermined.

I believe strongly that negotiation should be a win-win rather than a win-lose. Done well, negotiation can build goodwill and reinforce why the company extended you an offer. Done badly, it can lose goodwill and even cost you the offer.

For example, if you negotiate hard and really push the company, you might get a little more money. However, you're then going to walk into an organization where there are already negative feelings toward you.

I recently worked with a company that had two candidates they loved. The decision could have gone either way. The company was explicit during the process about the highest base salary they could offer. They decided to go with candidate A, who we had already calibrated to their range, and who had been happy to proceed. The candidate got the offer, which was exactly as was expected. Unfortunately, they were being advised by other people whispering in their ears to negotiate, which they did against our advice. When they tried to negotiate the salary, the company ended up withdrawing the offer. They made the same offer to the second candidate, who accepted on the spot.

Sometimes in negotiations, when companies say, "That's our final offer," it's their final offer. They're not trying to play games or shut down negotiation. They're saying it because it is as much as they can pay.

If you woo and wow them in the interview, there may be other things you can negotiate, such as sign-on bonus, start date, an extra week vacation, or incremental equity, but when companies are so explicit upfront about their salary, there's a reason.

STEP BY STEP

In terms of how and when to negotiate, these are the key steps I recommend:

- When you receive an offer, be very excited about the opportunity. Ask human resources, or whoever you're speaking with, to send you all relevant information to review, including the offer letter and benefits and relocation information, so you can read through all the details. In effect, you want to make sure you understand the total offer, and benefits are very much a part of that.
- Review everything thoroughly and come up with a list of informational questions. In the interview chapter, we discussed WIIFM questions: *What's in it for me*? I advised you to keep those questions in a folder as they came up. This is the time to take them out. Here are some good informational questions you might ask:
  - I am looking to join your company for the long term, and with that in mind, how do I think about success and growth in this role?
  - When do you pay out bonuses? What are bonus

payments based on? What has been the average payment percent in the last few years?

- ◦ If I start on this day, how much vacation would I get in the first year?
- ◦ What are the typical hours people work in my department?
- ◦ Is there ever flexibility to work from home?
- ◦ What are the typical raises at your company?
- ◦ When does 401(k) matching start?
- ◦ When does health insurance coverage start?

You could also ask to speak with the hiring manager to learn more about the role. You might also want to speak to one or two peers who report to the person you would work for, or perhaps to the person who was last in this role (assuming they are still with the company), in order to understand the work style.

When you have all your informational questions answered, and you know in your heart that you're really excited to join this company, it's time to negotiate. (Down the road, if you work with a quality recruiter, they will partner with you to negotiate effectively).

HOW TO NEGOTIATE

The most powerful tactic you can use is Yes...If.

It gives the team hiring you the incentive to fight on your behalf. When you are ready to negotiate, start the conversation in this way: "I love your company. This role is perfect. The culture fit is great. So, I want to say yes...if you can help me with a few things."

Then you lay out your few asks with a strong rationale as to why you need help. This might include details such as:

- A planned holiday: "I have a trip planned with my family. I'll be gone for this week and I want to make sure that it's okay with you. I could start earlier or take the vacation unpaid if needed."
- A changed start date: "I'd like to push it back one to two weeks as I can't resign until my drug test and background are cleared, and I need a few weeks to put my house on the market and move."
- If you're concerned about your sign-on bonus and salary, your rationale could be, "While I love this opportunity, I'm wondering if you can strengthen the offer somehow. Here's the reason why. I have a raise coming due in three months at my current company. With that impending raise, this is a lateral move. I'm also walking away from a half year of an earned bonus, which would equate to X dollars. I'm open to how you address this through the base or sign-on bonus. I'm open to really creative solutions because I want to make this work."
- If the total compensation package is lower than you

had anticipated, try offering creative options, such as a review in six months instead of the standard year, a sign-on bonus on your one-year anniversary that will help bridge the gap for your second year, or a guaranteed first-year bonus.

By negotiating in this manner, you're not negotiating *against* the company. By positioning it like this, you're working together to achieve the same goal. You want to be able to say yes, and they want you to be able to say yes. It is evident that you are partnering with them to come up with creative solutions that work for you both.

This is win-win negotiation.

NEGOTIATING FOR THE FIRST TIME

Realistically, for a student coming out of college or graduate school, the salary is set and non-negotiable. However, there are at times what are called "exploding" sign-on bonuses to motivate candidates to accept an offer early and get them off the market.

If that happens, you have to decide if the additional sign-on bonus is worth it, or if you want to see if you can get something better. Nobody but you can determine that.

At this time in your career, you often can't negotiate the

base or the bonus percentage, but you still might be able to negotiate a start date, planned holidays, or getting extra days off for moving. Sometimes when people finish graduate school, their healthcare goes until a certain date before they switch to COBRA for a couple of months. If your coverage for healthcare doesn't start until you've been at the company for thirty days, you could ask them for a sign-on bonus to cover out-of-pocket healthcare expenses.

One note about sign-on bonuses: Although they are sometimes offered to new graduates, it is not necessarily the case for experienced hires, unless they are leaving an earned bonus or equity behind. Don't expect a sign-on bonus just because you want one.

Whatever your asks, negotiation should always be win-win. If you're not comfortable with negotiating on your own, we are here to help. Contact us at http://www.igniteyourcareerbook.com/negotiation.

Your aim is to leave them even more excited about you after negotiations, due to your professionalism, your strong analytical thought process, and your collaborative negotiation style.

The same is true when it is time to leave a company, which will likely happen sooner or later in your career. You can part in a collaborative and constructive manner, as we'll see in chapter 10.

DOS AND DON'TS

Here are the dos and don'ts of negotiation:

DOS	DON'TS
Always lead with the positive: you want to be there; you are just asking for help to make it work.	Don't treat negotiation like a competition; it's not win-lose.
Approach negotiations in a win-win manner.	Do not negotiate until you're ready to accept an offer.
Listen to what they say and how they say it, so you don't lose goodwill.	Do not negotiate unless you want to be at the company.
Get your informational questions answered before you negotiate.	Don't be unrealistic. If you push too hard, you could lose the job or lots of goodwill.
Do the Yes...If when starting to negotiate.	
If they give you what you requested, do not ask for more.	
Have a strong rationale for your asks.	

CHAPTER 10

RESIGNING: IT'S A
SMALL WORLD

You have an offer from a new company. You've negotiated a win-win agreement, and you've accepted a new role. Yay! Once your background check and drug screen are completed, it is time to resign your present position, but for many people this is something they dread.

Resigning makes people uncomfortable, but it is an important part of the career-building process. Done the right way, it can build your goodwill and keep your options open down the road. It's a smaller world than you think.

The resignation process starts with a resignation letter. This is the last thing that will go in your employment file, so it should be simple, straightforward, brief, and positive. It should be addressed to either your supervisor or human resources.

I recommend not discussing your resignation with any colleagues before you submit your letter. The company should be the first to know, out of respect for them. The only exception might be if the new company asks that you provide references, in which case you might have to take one or two people into confidence, because you're asking them to serve as references.

Your resignation letter should have three paragraphs and you need not mention where you are going. In the first paragraph, you simply state that with this letter you are tendering your resignation as of today's date, and your final day will be two weeks later. You put that date in.

In the second paragraph, you say that you want to thank the company and the wonderful people you've encountered, learned from, and become friends with, and you hope to maintain these relationships for the long term.

The third paragraph is basically "thank you again for everything," and you sign and date it.

Then you set up a meeting to hand the letter to your boss or HR. The best way to approach the meeting is to say, "I have exciting and sad news. The sad news is that I'm going to be leaving the company. The exciting news is that I have a new opportunity that fits with my personal and professional needs, and I hope that you are excited for me."

COUNTEROFFERS NEVER WORK

It is possible that they will try to make a counteroffer. This is never a good idea. If you let them counteroffer and you still decide to leave, they will be even more frustrated. You will lose goodwill and they will be left with a bad taste in their mouth, because they went to bat for you and still ended up with nothing.

If you accept their counteroffer, whatever motivated you to explore external opportunities likely has not changed. If they offer you a little more money, it might feel good for a short while, but I don't know anybody who gets their job satisfaction from looking at their paycheck each month. You'll soon forget about the additional money, and you'll still be frustrated day in and day out. If you renege on an accepted offer, not only will you lose all goodwill at the new company, but they will never forget that you went back on your word.

In addition, you've shown your hand interviewing at another company and getting another job. That demonstrates that you're not loyal to your current organization. When it's time for promotions or raises, you're not going to be at the top of management's list. Studies show that within six months of accepting a counteroffer, more than 80 percent of employees have left the company anyway.

That's why you should never go out and get another offer to try to force your company to give you a pay raise or promotion. Instead of using a counteroffer as leverage, put a business case together as to why you deserve it and present it to your management before you start your job search. If they accept your case, that's awesome. If they say no, then at least you know where you stand. It's time to start a focused search.

KEEP IT PERSONAL

The world is much smaller than it used to be, with LinkedIn, Facebook, and email. Technology makes it more important than ever to leave a job with as much goodwill as possible, because word soon gets around. Everything you do has a long echo. Be mindful that the person you offend when you resign from this company might be the hiring manager in a company you want to join in five years' time.

When they ask about why you're leaving, hang your hat on something personal if you can, because that makes it easier for them to take, because they can't fulfill your personal need.

It's true that sometimes you'll be resigning from a company because you're miserable. The fit might not be right, the boss might not be right, the job might not be right. I'd advise against bringing any of that up in your resignation. Bringing up those things will just create ill will. You're moving on to something better. Kudos for you. But bite your tongue. You won't gain anything by being spiteful. Stick to your personal needs.

Take two of my candidates. One was working in the Southeast but had a severely ill family member. Getting back out West, where she had support on the personal front (she grew up there and her family still lived there) combined with a great job, was critical for her quality of life and her future. While the company she was leaving was disappointed, even devastated, they also understood and appreciated her situation. They were glad that she was going to have the support as she moved into the next phase of her life.

The other candidate was originally from the Midwest but was working in the New York Metro area. She had one child and was thinking about having a second. She and her husband decided they wanted to raise their family in the Midwest because of the lower cost of living and the higher quality of life there. She told her company, "I love you guys and I love what I've been able to do. But a great opportunity came up in the Midwest, and it feels right on all fronts for our growing family."

Putting it like that takes the sting out of your resignation for the company. Remember, they have emotion invested in the relationship, too.

Another thing I recommend is staying in touch with people after you leave the company via LinkedIn, Facebook, or other ways. In that way, you can continue building those relationships, because it is so much easier now to keep them strong than it was in the past. As we saw when we talked about networking, the larger your circle of contacts in your industry, the better.

HOW TO SAY NO

If you've followed the advice in this book and done your homework, you might be lucky enough to get multiple offers. This can happen when you are searching for a new job out of college or at different points in your career.

If this happens, you can only say yes to one company. You have to decline the others, but that does not mean you have to do it in a negative way. Declining in a timely and respectful manner will maintain goodwill for the long term. You never know when you're going to bump into the people you interviewed with again down the road. Make sure they think of you fondly. It's best to be "the one that got away."

The first way to accomplish this is never to start negotiations unless you want to join a company. Making them jump through hoops only for you to decline them anyway leaves a really bad taste in their mouth. It's bound to create ill will, and no one likes to think you are playing one offer off another.

Second, when you decline a company, thank them sincerely for the offer and tell them how much you enjoyed meeting them and how hard the decision was. Give a rationale that makes sense and share what changed since you started the process with them. No one likes to hear that you declined the position due to something you knew going into the process, such as geography, cost of living, or industry. They will still be disappointed, but they'll understand. Maybe another location is better for a family, or you've found a local role, or the other role has an equity stake with huge upside. Or you could explain that you want to stay at a training company in the short term, but that their company is where you might want to be in the long term. You'll reconnect in the future, hopefully when you'll have even stronger skills.

Write a thank-you email—or even better, a handwritten note—to the hiring manager and anyone else important in the process, telling them how much you enjoyed meeting them and that you would love to be on their team down the road.

Third, never ghost a company you interviewed with. You

cannot ignore them just because you are uncomfortable declining their offer. Always call them back and meet their timing. They will be disappointed when you decline, but they will also remember how classy and professional you were when you called.

The final thing: Never, ever decline via email. It's impersonal, unprofessional, and cowardly. You can follow up with an email, but you have to deliver the bad news in person on the phone.

You have a long career ahead of you, and leaving a company or declining an offer poorly is going to limit your long-term marketability. You never know where the people with whom you interact will work next. Bad impressions stick with people just as much as good impressions—if not more.

When I graduated from business school, I was lucky enough to have a full-time offer from Johnson & Johnson, where I had been an intern. I had an amazing experience and absolutely adored them, but Johnson & Johnson was not in my ideal location.

I ended up accepting an offer from Kraft in Chicago. Not only was the location far better; the Kraft culture and people also felt very similar to Johnson & Johnson.

I called to let Johnson & Johnson know I wasn't coming. I

explained why, but I was in tears because it broke my heart. It was so hard to turn them down. Still, I made sure they understood that it wasn't that I didn't love them or want to be there. It was only that the Chicago geography worked better. The result is that, decades later, I still have relationships with people from when I interned at J&J, because I really valued them then, and I still do now.

For me, that's one reflection of a successful career. Your career is made up of the people you meet and work with, and to genuinely value your colleagues and to feel valued in return is really the icing on the cake.

DOS AND DON'TS

Here are some of the dos and don'ts of resigning and declining.

DOS	DON'TS
Do be professional and respectful.	Don't ghost them.
Do resign or decline live on the phone rather than by email.	Don't say negative things about the company you are leaving.
Do follow up with a written note or email thanking them for everything.	Don't encourage a counteroffer; discourage one, if possible.
Do give them an authentic personal rationale they will appreciate.	Don't make your reason for declining something you already knew before you started the process.
Do be appreciative.	Don't be spiteful, personal, or resentful. You're moving on.

CONCLUSION

Not long ago, I was working with a candidate who was quite junior in his career, but who I thought had a good initial foundation of analysis and some marketing experience. His company was going through Chapter 11, so he was interviewing for a new job. He was a strong interviewer, and he got two offers, and the promise of two more in-person interviews. One offer was a lateral move to a strong training company. The other was with a tiny company, but it had an elevated job title.

Guess which offer appealed to his ego? His instinct was to go to a small company, where he would get promoted really quickly.

He asked for help with his decision, and I talked a lot about learn, do, leverage (see chapter 2). We discussed the tree analogy (see chapter 4), and how building a strong trunk was so critical. He really took it in.

The next day, he came back to me and said, "I want to build a sturdy trunk." He made the best decision for his long-term career potential and went to the strong training company, even though it was a higher cost of living there. His words to me were, "Now is the time to build a deep foundation. I have my entire career to focus on making money."

As a reader of this book, you probably know that I believe his decision will set him up for long-term success. He put his ego aside and took the long view.

You can also make the right career decisions, if you take the long-term view and can keep these analogies in mind:

- Your career is a marathon, not a sprint.
- Visualize your career like a tree.
- Be like a pool shark: Focus on winning the game, not making the easy shot.

As I explained early on in the book, it's important to be strategic about your career and mindful of how short-term choices will impact your long-term future. This strategy never gets stale. I urge you to revisit it throughout your career to help you keep on track and focused on the long term.

As an executive recruiter, I find it incredibly rewarding to assist individuals through the process of career development, growth, and transition at all levels, from SVP of marketing and chief marketing officer down to college graduates. Helping others optimize their career path is my life's calling.

OVER TO YOU

So, now you have your map and your tools. *Off you go!*

Build your foundation; develop superior skills; find a great culture fit; learn, do, leverage; and focus on your long-term goals. Invest in yourself, do your homework, network throughout your career, and treat others with kindness and respect. This world we live in is small, and your reputation is the core of who you are.

I wish you happiness and great success in this crazy journey called life.

Kris
XOXO

SERVICES TO HELP YOU ON YOUR CAREER JOURNEY

Resume Writing: www.igniteyourcareerbook.com/resumes

Negotiation: www.igniteyourcareerbook.com/negotiation

Interview Prep: www.igniteyourcareerbook.com/
interview-prep

Speaking Engagements: www.igniteyourcareerbook.com/
speaking-engagements

ACKNOWLEDGMENTS

I would like to give my thanks to my partners, Dixon Smith and Ken Dammeyer, for their support and insight while writing my book—it is truly a better book because you were part of the process. I deeply value and appreciate your partnership!

I would like to thank my family, who mean everything to me:

- To Jim—thanks for your love and support and for putting up with the early morning writing sessions and the endless chatter about the book...and for coming up with the name: *Ignite Your Career!*
- To Katie, Davey, and Sam—thanks for your love and support and for helping me stay focused on your generation and keeping me honest and grounded.

I would also like to thank my "coach," Doug Pearson, for giving me the "kick in the pants" to write this book that I have been thinking about for over fifteen years!

Thanks, too, to my colleagues at the O'Connell Group and the Pinnacle Society for your partnership and support on my journey and to both my clients and my candidates over the past twenty-five-plus years for igniting my career!

ABOUT THE AUTHOR

KRIS HOLMES is an executive recruiter and partner at O'Connell Group, a leading executive search firm in consumer marketing and market research. With more than twenty-five years of experience, she is also a member of the Pinnacle Society, the premier consortium of industry-leading recruiters in North America.

Kris has counseled tens of thousands of candidates in setting goals and leveraging their strengths. Before shifting to recruiting, Kris worked for a decade in consumer marketing with major corporations like Johnson & Johnson, Kraft Foods, and Ralston Purina. She's a graduate of Tufts University and has an MBA from the Kellogg School of Management at Northwestern.

Kris and her husband Jim are the proud parents of three wonderful kids and two happy yellow labs.